Dance to the Music of the Spirit
The Art of Discernment

DAVID LONSDALE sj

God is the lead dancer and the soul is the partner completely attuned to the rhythm and patterns set by the partner. She does not lead, but neither does she hang limp like a sack of potatoes.

Thomas Merton

Darton, Longman and Todd
London

First published in 1992 by
Darton, Longman and Todd Ltd
89 Lillie Road, London SW6 1UD

© 1992 David Lonsdale sj

ISBN 0–232–51948–X

Cover: Leigh Hurlock

Phototypeset by Intype, London
Printed and bound in Great Britain
at the University Press, Cambridge

To my brothers in the Society of Jesus,
and especially those who taught me discernment

Contents

Acknowledgements

I would like to express my sincere thanks in the first place to the Abbot and community of Mount St Joseph Abbey, Roscrea in Ireland, who allowed me to live as a guest at their monastery for four months in the summer of 1991. The peace of the Abbey and its surroundings, the framework of monastic prayer and the warm hospitality of the community provided me with a very congenial setting in which to begin writing this book. I would also like to thank all those people who have taken part in 'discernment workshops' with me. Their enthusiasm encouraged me to write this book and their contributions to the workshops have helped me to ground my reflections in real experience. I am grateful to Morag Reeve of Darton, Longman and Todd, especially for her patience as I failed to meet deadlines. Paula Mulryan IBVM, Frank Shephard and Paul Edwards SJ read the book in manuscript. I am very grateful to them for their helpful suggestions for improving the book, most of which I have acted upon. The mistakes are my own.

David Lonsdale SJ

Introduction – The way we were

I was brought up in the north of England in the immediate aftermath of the Second World War. When the war ended, I was less than a year old, and at the opening of the Second Vatican Council, I was not quite eighteen. My childhood and boyhood, therefore, were spent between those two great upheavals, each of which in its own way has affected my generation profoundly. My family were Roman Catholics in a working-class community which, during my early years at least, was struggling, on largely inadequate wages, to heal the scars of six years of war and to establish some semblance of normality and security. We lived in a fairly large market town with a port and an expanding motor industry. The staple industry was textiles. To have a 'trade', a small shop in a well-populated neighbourhood or a job at Leyland Motors, the local bus and truck factory, was to be in a good position. The community was thrifty, independent, hard-working, conservative in politics and religion, with a not undeserved reputation for stubbornness. Social and professional high-fliers, however, were looked on with suspicion, and I have rarely met another community that treats pretentiousness among its own members with such irony and even scorn. Many parents, having had few opportunities themselves, believed strongly in the value of education, but had little ambition for their children beyond a job that was

1

'steady' and secure rather than exciting, glamorous or even particularly highly paid.

Relative to the rest of Britain, the Roman Catholic community in the town was large. We were very aware of ourselves as 'Catholics' and for that reason as being in some very evident ways different from many of our neighbours. It was a community proud of its traditions, and of having 'kept the faith' while much of the rest of the country was turning 'Protestant'. It was also proud of its associations with the Roman Catholic martyrs; several of them had been born in nearby towns and villages and their names, Clitherow, Southworth, Arrowsmith, Osbaldeston, Oldcorne, Rigby, were those of our neighbours. Our Catholicism was English rather than Irish: our diocesan clergy were local men, trained in the northern seminaries or in Rome. Although socially the world of *Brideshead Revisited* and the Crouchback trilogy, with their country houses, servants and governesses, education, influential connections, private chapels and family chaplains seemed light years away from us, when I later read those novels, I found their Catholicism, with all its strengths and weaknesses, surprisingly familiar.

Being a Roman Catholic in those circumstances involved very definite patterns of behaviour: Mass and Benediction on Sundays, family rosary, observing Lent and Friday abstinence, sending children to Catholic schools, baptisms, marriages and funerals in Catholic churches with, in many cases, burials in a Catholic section of the town cemetery. In the neighbourhood in which we lived, we were aware of who were Catholics and who were not, and often of who were baptized Catholics but did not 'practise'. Inter-church or 'mixed' marriages always caused a stir in the community and the clergy preached against them regularly. To attend a service in a non-Catholic church, even a family wedding, was regarded as dangerous and wrong. While there was little open hostility between members of different churches, and Catholic and non-Catholic neighbours lived peacefully side by side, there was none the less a general awareness of a division. I also remember feeling envious at times of Protestant children: they did not have to go to church half so often – in fact it did not seem to matter whether they went to church or not – and they could eat sausages on any day of the week!

My generation, therefore, was formed in a mode of church membership which placed strong emphasis on institutional factors. Being a Catholic meant belonging to a church whose strong sense of identity was expressed in a powerful system of Catholic doctrines, structures, institutions, laws, practices, devotions and moral teachings. We thought of ourselves as 'good Catholics' in so far as we allowed that system to form us and to shape every aspect of our lives from birth to death.

The dominance of this form of church membership in the years before Vatican II gave a central place to rules and laws in our moral and spiritual formation. The lives of Roman Catholics were almost entirely controlled by laws, and I imagine that in this respect British Roman Catholicism reflected a world-wide experience. Apart from the Ten Commandments and the 'natural law', we were aware of the Commandments of the Church and Canon Law, which exerted a powerful influence. Furthermore, it was impressed upon us that there were rules and regulations capable of governing almost every imaginable situation in life; even, for example, detailed rules about the number of ounces of food permissible at each meal on fast days. When I was an altar server, liturgy was a matter of carrying out the ceremonial rules correctly and with dignity rather than a creative expression of the faith of a community. Morality was taught in the seminaries and preached from the pulpit on a basis of law. In discussions about morality, 'What is the law?' and 'Is it allowed?' were seen as more important questions than 'Is it good?'. The satire of Roman Catholic life in David Lodge's novel of those times *How Far Can You Go?* is accurate and effective.

Whatever the position outside the Roman Catholic church, our prayer life was largely devotional. Unlike their fellow-Christians in other churches, Roman Catholics had little direct contact with the Psalms and other biblical prayers or with the biblical text as a whole for purposes of meditation. Prayer books such as *The Key of Heaven* or *The Garden of the Soul* were full of devotional prayers for different occasions. I

3

was fortunate that in my last years at high school a Jesuit taught me and a few of my companions that there are other ways of praying besides reciting or reading prayers; but that was an exceptional privilege rather than a widespread practice. Many Catholics read through 'Devotions at Mass' in their prayer books or recited the rosary silently while Mass was being 'said' at the altar by a priest who stood for the most part with his back to the congregation. In my home parish on weekdays during the Marian months of May and October the priest 'said' Mass silently while the congregation recited the rosary aloud, pausing only for the moment of consecration and elevation. Once a week there was an evening Novena of 'Our Lady of Perpetual Succour', which included prayers addressed to the Virgin Mary, a sermon and Benediction of the Blessed Sacrament. On Sunday evenings, almost every Catholic church in the country had 'Devotions, sermon and Benediction'. In every Roman Catholic parish in the diocese in which we lived, on the first Sunday of May every year there was a procession in the church in the course of which a young girl aged seven or eight, in a long white dress, veil and train, placed a crown of flowers on the statue of Mary, with other children of the same age, dressed in white and blue, in solemn attendance. At the feast of Corpus Christi the same children, dressed this time in white and red, ceremoniously placed flower petals on the ground in front of the Sacrament carried in procession. These devotions and prayers fulfilled the necessary function of appealing to and nourishing people's affective and aesthetic needs, as did the elaborate ceremonial of the Mass.

I joined the Jesuits straight from secondary school two months before my nineteenth birthday. If this institutional form of church membership was the only one that most lay people knew, 'religious life' at that time also had a similar shape. It was part, and a highly respected part, of the same system. Our personal and communal lives were built upon a framework of structures and rules, and in that respect were typical of the religious life of both women and men at the time. When I joined the Jesuits in 1963, our Novice Master explained the Jesuit Constitutions to us as if they were a code of laws. One of his favourite sayings was, 'You keep the rule and the rule will keep you', and the basis of his classes was a commentary on the Constitutions written by a canon lawyer. As we learned more and more about the order we hoped to join, we discovered that apart from the Constitutions there were also what were called *The Common Rules*, a set of regulations supposed to govern Jesuit behaviour world-wide. Moreover, each province and each large house within the province had its own 'customs book', in which were written local rules for that particular province or house. We lived for the most part in large, highly structured communities. When I was studying philosophy, about 150 Jesuits, young and old, students and staff, lived and worked in the same college; we all dressed in the same way, and we prayed, ate, worked and took recreation at the same times. It was impressed upon us that a large part of being a 'good Jesuit', particularly during the years of training, was being able to live reasonably happily in this structured framework without being too noticeably different from one's companions. To my young eyes, acceptable eccentricity or nonconformity seemed to be a privilege granted only to those who were old and/or intellectually brilliant.

It would be a mistake to see this institutional mode of belonging to the church and the image of the church as a 'perfect society' which supported it as an aberration. It was a phase in the historical development of the church and of the church's understanding of itself. As such it had both positive and negative results. Postively, for example, it offered to people of every continent and every walk of life a coherent way of living based on the highest human values and ideals. It formed and supported throughout the world a vast number of – by any standards – outstandingly good people, disciples of Jesus, lay, religious and clergy. It is arguable also that the moral influence of Christianity in every major society and culture outside the Communist, Muslim and Hindu worlds has rarely been as great as it was in the first sixty years of this century. None the less, between the Second World War and the Second Vatican Council the pace of change in the world was increasing and inherited ways of being a Christian and a member of the church were found not to meet changing needs and aspirations. This prompted a search for forms of Christian living which would reflect more fully the true values of the gospels and offer a more adequate response to the demands of the modern world.

It was after I had been a Jesuit for about five years that I was gradually introduced to a way of being a Christian which, for me at least, had an emphasis that was quite new. Several factors contributed to this change. Vatican II opened the way for all Roman Catholics to an understanding of the church which was both different from and far more exciting than the old 'institutional' one which my generation and I had inherited from the last century. Younger members of religious orders and congregations were increasingly questioning the inherited theory, structures and practices that moulded their lives. At the same time, when, with the encouragement of the Council, religious orders and congregations became engaged in studying their own roots and original inspirations, they often found there, to their surprise, a form of Christian discipleship which had a very different shape and emphasis from the institutional one which was then dominant.

For me, however, the changes that were then going on had also a more personal dimension. By way of spiritual direction, casual conversations and the newly rediscovered guided retreats, a Jesuit called Michael Kyne taught me a new way of being a Christian and a Jesuit. He showed me little by little that Christian discipleship is more than allowing certain laws and structures to shape one's life; that my own and other people's history, experience, gifts, desires, feelings, understanding, ideas and 'inspirations' are places in which the Holy Spirit is present and at work for the service of the kingdom and for 'the building up of the body of Christ' (Eph. 4:12); and that whoever we are, lay, cleric or religious, if we reflect in a certain way on these elements of our experience and act on that reflection, we allow the Spirit of God to shape us in the image of Christ through the ordinary events of everyday life. In a word, he taught me the art of discernment. I was also surprised to learn, moreover, that this way of being a Christian is in fact at the heart of the legacy bequeathed to the Jesuits and the church by Ignatius Loyola, the order's founder. From that time on I have believed that Christian discernment offers us a practical way of living as sons and daughters of the Father and brothers and sisters of Jesus Christ which is particularly suited to today's conditions.

I have begun this book with part of my own story because it seems to me that my experience of growing up as a Roman Catholic in Britain in the years between the Second World War and the Second Vatican Council is by no means untypical. History and local culture had given Roman Catholicism in that small area of Britain its individual features. None the less, this experience both of Roman Catholicism and of relationships between the different Christian churches was reproduced in many other places in Europe and North America, and the forms of Christianity that it encouraged were exported to every continent.

1

Setting the scene

Christian spirituality, the life of discipleship, has been well described as 'life in the Spirit as sons and daughters of the Father and brothers and sisters of Jesus Christ'.[1] When we try to live this discipleship, we find ourselves engaged in making choices, both in the circumstances of every day and at the crucial turning points of life. Our choices are what give shape and direction to our lives. The value of discernment is that it offers us a way of making Christian choices, of following the leading of the Spirit of God in the decisions that we make.

THE PRESENT NEED FOR DISCERNMENT

In the church in which we live at present, discernment is a much-needed gift. We are witnessing, in the Roman Catholic church in particular, a shift from an institutional form of church membership, some of the features of which I have described in my introduction, to a far more participatory mode of membership. Here the emphasis is placed on such values as, for example, personal commitment rather than belonging by birth or convention, the universal call to holiness of all the baptized, co-responsibility among the members for decisions which affect their own lives and the community as a whole, sharing of ministries among both lay and ordained members, and a desire to change radically a hierarchical structure which is seen as in many respects discriminatory. In this chapter I wish to show that this continuing shift of emphasis makes a sound practice of individual and group discernment a matter of urgency in the church. This will mean exploring further some features of a participatory form of discipleship as a way of setting the scene for our later discussion of discernment.

My reflections in this chapter focus mainly on features of Roman Catholic life, partly because I am taking my own experience, limited as it is, as a starting point for more general considerations. Some of the changes that have taken place in the Roman Catholic church, such as developments in the liturgy, have had their effects and their counterparts in other Christian communions. On the other hand, it may be that in other sections of the Christian church some of the conditions for the practice of discernment were already more firmly in place before the era of change that is associated in the Roman Catholic communion with Vatican II. The rest of this chapter, however, will be devoted to discussing four factors which seem to me to have led to a rediscovery of the need for the ancient Christian skills of discernment of spirits in a largely Roman Catholic context. Members of other churches will be able to reflect on them in the light of their own and to some degree different ecclesial experience.

MODELS OF THE CHURCH

In the church there is always, and probably always has been, a continuous tension between 'institutional' and 'charismatic' elements. On the one hand the Spirit of God is present in and works through the church's structural elements: the ministry of the ordained members, the authority of the church's teaching office and hierarchy, the sacraments rightly 'administered', church order, all those features which are said to belong to the church as a divinely appointed 'institution'. On the other hand, the Spirit of God is by no means confined to these institutional elements, but is also present and active in the experience, 'charisms', ideas, desires, creativity and projects of individuals and groups in the church which do not form part of those institutional structures.

The view of the church with which generations who grew

9

up before Vatican II were imbued was of a well-ordered society with a central authority: a strictly hierarchical, divine institution set apart from (and to a large extent opposed to) 'the world'. According to this way of understanding the church, the Spirit of God is seen as operating almost exclusively through the hierarchy and the sacraments. Fidelity to the Spirit tends to be interpreted as a matter of orthodoxy in belief, obedience to church authority and the moral law, 'receiving' the sacraments as 'channels of grace', and allowing one's life to be shaped by the church's structures and institutions.

When this view of the church predominates, there tends to be little scope for personal discernment, understood as the capacity of an individual or a group within the church to respond to the inner, personal promptings of the Spirit and to read 'the signs of the times' – those trends and events in our own age which seem to speak to us of God's purposes for the world. In fact church authorities might look upon such personal experiences with some suspicion as being 'unsafe' and likely to mislead. In this way the art of personal discernment tends to be moved to the periphery of the Christian life, while the balance between institution and charism in the church is weighted in favour of the former.

No single 'model' of the church, however, encapsulates all that the church is. The image of the church as a hierarchical institution is only one among several: the church can also be understood as the Body of Christ, a communion and community of disciples of Jesus, a servant, a herald, and so on. Together all these different 'models' help us to approach a fuller understanding of the mystery which the church is.

One of the most refreshing and liberating aspects of the recent developments in the church's understanding of itself is the rediscovery of the importance of the 'charismatic' elements. By this I do not mean only what later came to be called 'charismatic renewal', which is only one manifestation of the charismatic, but something much broader. What many of our new and rediscovered images of the church express is the fact that grace, the Spirit of God active in the world, works in and through all the members of the church (and outside the limits of the visible church as well); and that the call to be a Christian is an invitation to day-by-day fidelity to the Spirit of God as sisters and brothers of Jesus Christ. The presence and action of the Holy Spirit, therefore, in the gifts, experience, choices and actions of individuals and groups outside the church's institutional structures, have a contribution to make that is crucial to the church's well-being. Since all the gifts that the Spirit gives are for the sake of building up the body of Christ, this charismatic element has an essential part to play if the church is truly to reflect the values of the gospel in the service of the reign of God in the modern world.

In this context, therefore, the arts of personal and group discernment at the present time are being developed as a very necessary response to a renewed understanding of the place of the 'charisms' of individuals and groups. If the Holy Spirit is active throughout the church (and beyond), individuals and groups need to be able to differentiate the voice of the Spirit from all the other voices clamouring for attention. If we are called to join in the dance to the music of the Spirit, we also need to be able to distinguish the Spirit's music from the other melodies that float upon the air. Discernment offers a way of distinguishing between true and false gifts, between personal gifts that build up the body of Christ and those that do not, between the movements of the Spirit of God and those which are opposed to the Spirit. In the context of our present experience of the church, therefore, discernment is a necessary gift, because it offers a way of being faithful to the Spirit of God in everyday life.

PERSONAL FREEDOM

Another area of significant change in the last generation has to do with personal freedom. Institutional modes of church membership emphasized conformity and uniformity of belief and practice. Little attention was paid in practice to genuine personal freedom, though freedom of conscience was acknowl-edged in principle. In the areas of doctrine and moral

11

teaching, experts argued over matters in which it was accepted that there could be differences of opinion, but these matters were relatively small and few. Lay people, being largely untrained in theology, were not expected to exercise genuine freedom of conscience even about those disputed questions. Their part was to accept what they were told from the pulpit and in the confessional. The ideal for the lay person was a 'rightly informed' conscience rather than freedom to explore, but sadly all too often 'rightly informed' meant no more than being taught to accept and obey what was handed down by those in authority. Genuine pluralism was rare in theology, morals or church order.

In this area too the church's understanding of itself has changed significantly since Vatican II. Since the Council, in response to the gospel and to its perceptions of the contemporary aspirations of humanity, reasserted the value of personal freedom, responsibility and commitment, Roman Catholic Christians are rediscovering personal freedom in areas of life almost unimaginable thirty years ago. In matters of belief, we see a growing willingness to accept that there can be more than one valid theological approach to issues which previously had seemed closed. In forms of prayer, worship, lifestyle and morality we see a respect for personal responsibility and freedom and a growing scope for choice, initiative, experiment and creativity, both individually and collectively.

In this context discernment is both possible and necessary. It implies that we have both the ability and the space to exercise genuine freedom in decisions that touch upon the shape and direction of our lives as Christians. In the present situation in the church, discernment is possible because there are genuine options in different areas of life and a real possibility of choosing between them. And the development of the art of discernment is necessary because, if there are choices to be made, we need to have a process which enables us to make them well, under the leadership of the Spirit of God.

THE RULE OF LAW

Another shift that is taking place in our experience of what it means to be a Christian has to do with changing perceptions of the nature and place of law in the life of the church. In the introduction to this book I described how the dominant institutional mode of church membership thirty years ago and more placed a heavy emphasis on rules and laws, so that there were regulations covering almost every imaginable aspect of life. Moreover, in practice among Roman Catholics the usual approach to making moral decisions was to find the appropriate rule or law and to apply it. This was supported by the current view among theologians of the time that making good decisions means finding the right rule or general principle for a particular situation and applying it correctly. In that context, if discernment has any meaning at all, it is as a special process of decision-making for those comparatively rare circumstances, such as the choice of a personal vocation, in which no general norm or principle applies.

The recent and continuing rediscovery of different ways of understanding the church, and the contemporary recognition of the value of personal freedom, mean that laws are neither so all-pervasive nor so powerful as they used to be in the church's life. At the same time, as the power of rules and law has diminished, the scope for responsibility, personal choice and creative action for both individuals and groups within the church has grown.

From this perspective too, therefore, our contemporary need for an adequate theory and practice of discernment is an urgent one. If I am driving a train along a track, provided that the machinery and the rails are in good working order and that I and other drivers obey the signals and drive correctly according to the principles and rules set out in the driver's manual, I will reach my destination without mishap. Here, the scope for initiative, creativity or personal choice is quite limited. That is an image which illustrates one view of the Christian life. And yet if we are to believe the gospel portrait, Jesus was original, creative and free in his service of God and people, and at the same time rooted in and faithful to tradition. It would be wrong to banish these qualities from our practice of Christian discipleship, so that it becomes little more than a code of laws. If we want to keep the image of a journey, perhaps walking in the mountains offers a more satisfying image of the Christian life. There are maps which give essential information, books, films and videos by those who have gone before and a variety of paths to choose from. When, with whom and by what route we travel is a matter of personal choice. God is a constant companion, but a successful journey could also depend on our wisdom in assessing wind and weather and in using a compass.

'PERFECTIONIST' APPROACHES TO SPIRITUALITY

When a sculptor is carving a statue from a block of wood, she has an idea – or an ideal – in her mind of the statue as she hopes it to be when it is finished, and drawings and perhaps even detailed plans of the projected work with accurate measurements and proportions to scale. She also has her knowledge of the wood, its idiosyncrasies and its potentialities; and she will probably learn more about this as she carves.

This image may be used to illustrate different approaches to spirituality. One approach, which we may call 'perfectionist', is by way of focusing mainly on the ideal to be striven for and the means to be used in pursuit of the ideal: the ideal statue already present in the sculptor's mind and the carving tools which will produce it. The Roman Catholicism of thirty years ago favoured such a 'perfectionist' approach. The teaching hierarchy of the church drew from the tradition and set before its members both the ideals of 'Christian perfection' appropriate to different 'states of life', cleric, religious, lay, married or single, and the means to be used in the effort to reach and practise those ideals. The task of the individual members of the church was to strive for those ideals by use of the means the church offered: prayer, penance, asceticism, the sacramental life, obedience to the moral law and the rules of church membership, cultivation of the virtues proper to one's position in the church. 'Don't tell me how you're feeling, just do what I say' is a not wholly inaccurate summary of the process.

In the last twenty years, in both spirituality and ethics, we have developed a very different approach to living the Christian life. In preaching, education, retreats, workshops and courses in spirituality, far more attention is being paid to an individual person's own experience, and in particular to those fundamental responses to other people and to God which reveal who each person really is. We rightly focus far more than before on the shape, quirks and unique potentialities of the wood that the sculptor has chosen to use; we pay far more attention to the basic material of the human person with her or his history, capacities, needs and desires, as a member of the community of faith. In other words, we are now in a better position to recognize the need that we have for discernment if our Christian spirituality is to be adequate to our needs. For discernment involves fostering Christian growth by giving attention to an individual's or a group's unique history, experience, aspirations, desires and feelings in relation to the 'signs of the times' and the gospel. In terms of our 'sculptor', it means recognizing that the desired image arises out of a particular block of wood and therefore paying careful attention to such factors as the age, texture, history and idiosyncrasies of the wood the sculptor uses.

That does not mean, however, that we have lost sight of the Christian ideal. We continue to recognize that in the incarnation, life, death and resurrection of Jesus we have a powerful statement both of who God is and of what humankind is called by God to be. But we have also come to realize once again that the image of Christ that each of us is called to be lies within us. It is precisely our deepest desires and our past and present responses to the God whom the world discloses to us which are the seeds of growth and the best indicators we have of the direction in which God is calling us.

DEVOTION

Before the Second Vatican Council, the prayer life of most Roman Catholics meant reading or reciting devotional prayers written by other people. If any significant place was allowed for discernment of spirits in their prayer lives, it was under unusual circumstances and for people regarded as exceptional. An individual who had reached what was seen as an 'advanced' stage of prayer, which might involve experiences quite out of the ordinary, would need guidance and discernment at the hands of a skilled spiritual director. It was for the spiritual director to decide whether these experiences were genuine and beneficial and to give advice on how to respond to them. Similarly, claims about extraordinary revelations, 'visions' and apparitions were subjected to ecclesiastical authority as a test of their validity and value. But clearly these were exceptional cases.

The disappearance or drastic reduction of devotions in Roman Catholic life after Vatican II left a vacuum in the lives of very many people. There was suddenly nothing that could meet their affective and aesthetic needs. Since that time, however, many have been in a position to turn instead to new kinds of religious art, icons, music and dance and to new ways of praying and worship which do answer their needs. In the context of a discussion of the place of discernment in daily Christian living, it is perhaps important to note in particular two features of these changes. The first is the fact that by refashioning the liturgy and discovering meditation and contemplation as a way of prayer for the many and not just for the privileged few, a growing number of people are able to have direct and frequent contact with the biblical word of God. And the second is that we have rediscovered the value of prayer that is spontaneous and receptive, forms of prayer that involve listening as well as talking. Each of these developments helps to create a climate that fosters the practice of discernment in everyday life. For on the one hand discernment involves allowing one's life to be shaped by a personal appropriation of the word of God. And on the other hand, if discernment is to be effective, it calls for a form of prayer that involves an open and receptive stance before God, an attitude of listening. Meditation on the biblical text offers a privileged place in which to meet and to listen to that God.

CONCLUSION

In this chapter I have described a series of shifts in our experience of Christian living: significant changes in our understanding of what the church is, in the value that we place on personal freedom and responsibility, in our approaches to morality and spirituality and in the life of prayer. Though I have focused mainly on Roman Catholic experience, these changes also no doubt have their effects and counterparts in varying degrees in the lives of the members of other Christian churches and groups. My hope is that this description will help to illustrate the fact that the development of the art of Christian discernment at the present time is both a matter of necessity and an immensely valuable contribution to the life of the church. The shifts in understanding and practice that I have described offer us the possibility of enriching the life of the church in this way.

The developments that I have described, however, have not stopped but still continue. If anything, in the church as well as in society the pace of change is accelerating. In this setting, if our lives are shaped by the choices that we make, we need a method which will enable us to make them well. Discernment is necessary because it helps us both to see the path of true Christian discipleship in circumstances which are rapidly changing, and to make creative choices accordingly. Discernment engages us in the dance to the music of the Spirit. It puts us in touch with the Spirit of God who is present in these changes and who through them invites us to cooperate in the creation of a world in the image of God.

1 Cf. Walter Principe, 'Towards Defining Spirituality', *Sciences Religieuses / Studies in Religion*, vol. 12, no. 2, pp. 127–141.

2

The context of discernment

Discernment, whether in the course of everyday life or at times of particularly important decisions, has to do with making good choices. We always make choices, not in the abstract, but within a range of particular options and within a certain setting of time and place. Even if these are obvious statements, nevertheless in a discussion of the theory and practice of discernment it is important that we take note of them. The setting in which we make our choices is not simply a passive backdrop. On the contrary, the circumstances in which we are placed when we have decisions to make have a very powerful influence on the whole process of choosing. The purpose of this chapter, therefore, is to describe some of the principal factors, social, cultural, religious and personal, which are present in any setting in which we practise discernment, and to discuss some of the ways in which these factors affect the decision-making process. I also put forward in this chapter a basic theological framework within which discernment can be understood and appreciated.

THE SETTING OF DISCERNMENT: GOD'S CREATION

There is quite a dramatic change taking place at the present time in the attitudes of many Christians towards the created universe and the place of humankind within that universe. An older, more traditional understanding of this sees humanity as endowed with a God-given vocation to master and control the universe and everything in it. This view is often supported

18

by a particular interpretation of the Genesis creation story. The blessing, 'Be fruitful, multiply, fill the earth and conquer it. Be masters of the fish of the sea, the birds of heaven and all living animals on the earth' (Gen. 1:28) and the story of Adam naming 'all the cattle, all the birds of heaven and all the wild beasts' (Gen. 2:20) have long been seen as conferring on Adam, as a representative of humanity as whole, power over the rest of creation with the right to use and exploit the world's resources. The Christian theories of 'responsible stewardship' that developed from this encouraged the human race to exercise its mastery and its 'consumers' rights' over the rest of creation for the common good of humanity as a whole and not for the sake of promoting the selfish interests of any one individual or group. One constant feature of these theories, however, is that they accept the belief that we as human beings are masters of the world and have the right to exploit and consume the riches of the earth for the sake of our own well-being and development.

In the last few years a new kind of awareness has arisen which has challenged this position. For a long time, perhaps naïvely, we have taken for granted that industrial and techno-logical progress are beneficial, having no significant negative results. Now, however, we are becoming increasingly aware of their possible destructive effects both on those elements of our environment, such as the rain forests and the ozone layer, which maintain the balance necessary to support life, and on the human race itself. Writers on this subject point to the devastating effects of industrialization, modern economics and technological development: 50,000 nuclear warheads that could destroy the whole earth several times over; the whole-sale pollution and destruction of the atmosphere and the natural environment on every continent; a system of distribut-ing food, social goods and services that results in a thousand million underdeveloped and starving human persons.

This present state of our planet is said to be linked to the fact that we have been brought up in cultures that neglected or exploited the cosmos for the sake of an exclusive and uncritical focus on the human. We have concentrated so much on the development of the human species – or, to be more

19

accurate, on the development in certain directions of that portion of the human species that has access to the world's wealth – that the survival of the earth itself as a life-supporting environment is under threat. The urgent need, therefore, is to correct this destructive trend before it is too late: to emphasize, not the separateness and difference but the unity and interdependence between the human species and the rest of the created universe; to acknowledge the lessons of history which teach us that to look for the good of humanity at the expense of the rest of the planet actually destroys both the human species and the environment which supports it; to see the cosmos, therefore, as a unity with a single history and destiny, and to take steps to provide for the well-being of the whole created world. To carry this programme through would necessarily also involve an economic order that ensured a more just social distribution of goods and services across the world.

There is a broad range of attitudes on this matter. At one end of the spectrum stands the view that the present state of the earth and its inhabitants is more or less acceptable. At the other end is the belief that the dominant Western culture is so mechanistic, dualistic, patriarchal, anthropocentric and militaristic, and the planet is already in such a physically and morally catastrophic condition, that nothing short of radical transformation will do.

Our attitudes towards the whole of God's creation are an influential, if often unrecognized, factor in the setting in which we make our decisions at the present time. In the course of discernment, whether in daily life or at a time of making major choices, our position on this moral spectrum makes a great difference to the decisions that we make. This is obvious, for example, in the case of politicians or other powerful people whose economic or environmental policies have a direct effect on the lives of large numbers of people. What is not so obvious, however, is that many of even the 'ordinary person's' choices about, for example, work, political allegiance, use of wealth and property, shareholding in companies or personal and family lifestyle, are also shaped, at least in part, by their attitudes towards the created world and the place of the human species within that world. If I believe, for example, that human beings have a right ruthlessly to exploit and consume the resources of the earth, without any concern for effects such as global warming or pollution of the atmosphere, I will choose options, even in my day-to-day life, that are markedly different from those of another person who believes that care for the earth and the whole of God's creation is of paramount importance.

THE SETTING OF DISCERNMENT: SOCIETY AND CULTURE

Discernment has to do with choices made within a living relationship with God. Our choices embody certain values, and we inevitably derive these values from the particular society and culture to which we belong. In this way society and culture have a major influence upon the options we choose and the means by which we choose them.

One of the dominant features of Western society and culture at the present time is a widespread tendency to emphasize as a major value the good of the individual person, even at the expense of the good of the community or of society as whole. Partly as a result of this focus in our culture, we also run the risk in Christian decision-making of an excessive individualism. We can focus on the individual to such an extent that we forget that individuals exist only because they are created and nourished by social and cultural relationships, structures and institutions, and are dependent on them for survival and quality of life. Relationships, structures and institutions are the soil in which individuals grow and flourish; if they are taken away, individuals are in danger of dying. Moreover, besides making good choices for ourselves as individuals, we also have a responsibility to society: for considering and contributing to its well-being; for helping to shape its values; for trying to ensure that it is a setting in which all who belong to it are able to live in a way that matches their dignity as sons and daughters of the Father and brothers and sisters of Jesus Christ. The Christian faith is not a private affair, which has to do only with 'myself and God', but has an inseparable social dimension.

When we ignore these facts or do not allow them to have an influence on the processes by which we make choices as Christians, we are in danger of shaping our lives in a way that is harmful for ourselves as individuals, for others and for society. It is a path to destruction because God's love is for all, God's concern is for the well-being of all. In the wisdom of God's plan, individuals find their true fulfilment and become what God intends them to be, not in isolation or by considering only themselves, but as members of a society and a culture and through the right ordering of relationships, structures and institutions in society.

At the same time, in Christian discernment, it is very important that our choices are not wholly and uncritically determined by the society and culture in which we live, but that we are in a position to subject those values and the society and culture which offer them to us to criticism and challenge. After all, the word of God, which is the foundation of our Christian commitment, is more than a human wisdom and a human set of values. Throughout Judaeo-Christian history, those who, like Jesus and the prophets, believed they were called to receive the word of God and to be guided by it, have claimed the privilege of taking a critical stance towards certain features of their own society. They have subjected society and culture to criticism on the basis of the word of God and offered an alternative set of values and structures which in many cases were markedly different from those which society provided at that time. Since discernment, there-fore, means allowing God's received revelation to set the agenda for our choices, it is essential that we also have the opportunity for the same kind of freedom. If we are to main-tain our Christian integrity, it is vital that we are in a position to challenge, when appropriate, the values offered to us by the society and culture to which we belong, and to allow our choices to be made on the basis of a different set of values, which we derive from our understanding and appropriation of the word of God. When this happens, though society and culture do provide us with values and structures which we embody in our choices, we also have the freedom and the means to be different, to offer alternatives, to be 'prophetic'.

THE SETTING OF DISCERNMENT: THE CHURCH, COMMUNITY OF FAITH

Christian discernment usually takes place in the setting of a community of faith. Being a Christian does not mean life in isolation; it means being a member of a community, the people of God. From the beginning, God's gift of salvation has been offered, not to individuals in isolation from each other, but to a people, and the church is always a social reality in ceaseless interaction with the surrounding 'world'. Christian discipleship therefore, far from being primarily an individual matter, is first and foremost the response to God's offer of reconciliation and salvation to a people and to the whole world.

In practice, being a Christian usually means belonging to several different but interrelated communities at once: a family, a parish, a diocese, the church as a whole; and within those structures, perhaps a prayer group, for example, or an RCIA group, a lay community, a religious congregation, a network of like-minded friends spread across the world, and so on. The forms in which we participate in the life of all these different communities and the extent of our involvements in them are of course enormously varied. From the point of view of our present discussion of discernment, however, it is important to recognize that when we make choices and try to follow the leading of the Spirit, we do not act as individuals in isolation but as participating members of a number of overlapping faith communities. Discerning the Spirit is both a corporate and an individual activity. These communities provide part of the total framework within which we make discerning choices.

Our various communities help to shape our choices in a variety of ways. By forming our minds and hearts, the traditions, beliefs, norms and practices of the church to which we belong, like society and its culture, help to make us the

23

people that we are and to determine the values by which we live. Moreover, the local communities in which we have a part to play also rightly influence our choices in more immediate and tangible ways. For lay people, for example, the communities that play a vital part in discernment might be, in varying degrees, their family and friends, the local parish or diocese, or perhaps a group or association of which they are members. For a priest the important community which has a bearing on his choices might be his parish or diocese. For religious the institute or congregation of which they are members has a very important role and voice in any discernment, however 'personal' it may be.

Moreover, the relationship between the individual and the community in discernment is a two-way dialogue. On the one hand the community helps to shape our values, the decisions which arise from them and therefore our individual lives. On the other hand, just as we have a responsibility to help to determine for the common good the values and structures of the society in which we live, so also we have a duty to help to shape the church or other faith communities to which we belong and which nourish and support us. We fulfil this duty when the good of the community is a significant factor in all our choices.

The pervading influence of a sometimes exaggerated individualism suggests that it is important at the present time to recognize that the faith communities to which we belong have an essential part to play in personal discernment. In communities whose structures have for a long time been tight and authoritarian, discovering the possibility of 'personal discernment' sometimes seems like an exhilarating emancipation into previously undreamed-of personal freedom. This is an instance in which, in the name of freedom and as a reaction to the restrictions of structures now seen as oppressive, one can easily slip into an excessive individualism and look for 'the will of God' in isolation rather than in partnership with the community and its leaders. To try to find 'the will of God' in isolation in this way can easily lead to delusion and even disaster; it is like a husband trying to find the will of God in isolation from his wife and family rather than in partnership with them. Discerning the Spirit, even in personal matters, is in a real sense both a corporate and a personal process in which the community of faith has a proper role to play.

Suppose, for example, Mary is a member of a religious congregation and she feels that the time has come for a change of ministry. Formerly the members of the congregation used to be assigned ministries by the Provincial, with little if any personal consultation. That, however, has changed and in recent years the sisters have been encouraging each other to practise 'personal discernment'. In regular dialogue with a spiritual director, who is not a member of her congregation, Mary works through a process of discernment. She enjoys this new-found freedom and eventually approaches her Provincial with the results of her discernment. When the Provincial demurs, she states quite adamantly that this is without question the ministry to which she has 'discerned' she is being called by God. At this stage, while Mary's discernment may be open and honest within certain limits, up to this point she has made her choice in isolation from the community. If her decision-making process is to be truly discerning, it has to be in partnership with the community to which she belongs, and she has a responsibility to consider, not only her own good as she perceives it, but also the good of the community. That is how the Spirit works in the church.

While it is true that good discernment involves a partnership between individuals and the significant communities to which they belong, none the less it is also vital that the lives of the members are not so controlled and determined by those communities that they have no effective personal freedom. If discernment is to be fruitful, individual members (and small groups) need to have space for personal freedom within those larger communities. This is vital because the one Spirit of God works through individuals and local communities as well as through the whole church; through lay as well as through ordained members. We have seen in the previous chapter that a strongly authoritarian church leaves little room for individual freedom in discernment, especially for lay people. The authoritarian structures can be so restricting that the church's members are deprived of effective power of choice, and there is then a grave danger of quenching the Spirit in individuals, groups or local churches.

In practice, participatory forms of church membership, rather than institutional or authoritarian forms, create the best conditions for good discernment. A participatory form of membership means that people are members of a particular church or community by choice and commitment rather than by birth or social convention. It involves a vision of the church which recognizes both in theory and in practice that the Spirit of God is present and active in all the members, so that the search for 'what the Spirit is saying to the churches' is a matter in which all collaborate in various ways, and not simply the responsibility of a central teaching office or an ordained hierarchy.

It would be unrealistic, however, to suppose that this dialogue is an immediate guarantee of unanimity and harmony within a community of faith. Neither authoritarian nor participatory models of church membership guarantee that the search for fidelity to the Spirit will always be an unruffled and harmonious process. In fact one would more readily expect this search inevitably to involve tension, conflict and discord, given the people and the factors involved. Any process of discernment for an individual or for a group involves tension between opposite states of feeling, and that is a potential source of conflict. Moreover, in a community, whether small or large, there are legitimately different points of view, perspective and convictions. There is also the possibility that some of the people involved in searching for the Spirit, including the leaders in a community, are subject to laziness, blindness, self-interest, resistance to opposed points of view, a sectarian outlook, a desire to maintain the institution and the status quo at all costs, and many other ills which the flesh is heir to. All these have the potential for creating tension and conflict.

Surely the truth of the matter is that these factors and the tension they produce, far from being insurmountable obstacles to fidelity to the Spirit, may in fact be precisely the means by which God has ordained that a community should discover what the Spirit is saying. Outstanding Christians such as Catherine of Siena, Francis of Assisi, Teresa of Avila, Ignatius Loyola, Mary Ward and many others in our own time have found themselves at odds with the church's leaders, but the conflict has eventually proved creative and fruitful. In practice, working together in discernment in an honest search for the leading of the Spirit inevitably involves recognizing different points of view and varieties of feeling, acknowledging differences, obstacles and resistances, clarifying intentions, and so on, in a common enterprise. The tensions and struggles that thus arise may in fact be seen as the proper process given to us by God to enable us gradually, if often painfully, to be healed in mind, heart and spirit and, as individuals and communities, to discern the Spirit and follow the Spirit's lead. In this way, the tensions and struggles that we experience in an honest search for the truth become a source of life and creativity and help us to grow.

THE SETTING OF DISCERNMENT: PERSONAL AND COMMUNAL FAITH HISTORY

Discernment has to do with giving shape and direction to our lives in the present as we move into the future. But our lives already have a shape and direction given to us by the circumstances of the past and the choices we have made in those circumstances. The past, in the sense both of our personal past and of the corporate past we have shared with others, has made us what we are.

Another important aspect, therefore, of the setting in which we make choices in response to the Spirit of God, is our awareness of our personal and communal faith history. By 'faith history' I mean the story of each of us, in the personal, social, cultural and ecclesial circumstances in which we have lived, seen in relation to God. Each person's own history can be read as the story of a relationship with God, even when for a period of time God was unknown, forgotten or ignored. The fact that we give little attention to God does not mean that God gives little attention to us. Whether we are aware of God or not, our whole lives are lived in relation to God,

27

because God is the living source of life and of all that we have, even if we do not allude to that fact. The faith history of any individual or group is a story of two kinds of responses to God: moments in which we have sought union with God and answered God's invitations with love and generosity, and other moments in which we have turned away from God, deficient in love. It is history of both grace and sin.

The communal dimension of our faith history should also not be forgotten. The streams of our different lives are not isolated from each other, as if flowing in parallel lines; they intersect and the waters intermingle. God deals with us as a people and as individuals within that people. Our individual histories are elements in the greater story of God's people. The world, the society, the culture and the church in which we live also have a history with which our own personal history is closely bound up. Some of the choices that our predecessors and we ourselves made, whether in positive or negative response to God's love, created systems, structures and institutions which remain with us. That history has helped to create us. Looking at, reflecting on and appropriating in faith that broader, shared history, then, is also an important factor in discernment, because it is the story of God's covenant with his people. It shows us how the God of faithfulness has dealt with us in the past as a people, and that too has an important bearing on the choices we make in the present.

Telling the story of our lives in relation to God, and reflecting on the different aspects of it, help us to recognize where and how God has been and continues to be present and active in that story. This is an aid to discernment. First of all the pattern of the presence and action of God in our lives in the past offers a guide to where God is leading us here and now, which is precisely what we are concerned about in the practice of discernment. Our personal life is more like a winding stream than a series of isolated pools. There is a continuous flow between God's dealings with us in the past and God's leading of us into the future. This obviously does not mean that the present and the future are, or will be, exactly the same as the past; history and growth, after all, are not simply repetitions of the same events or circumstances. None the less, because each of us remains the same person through all change, there is continuity between the ways in which God deals with us throughout our lives. At the same time, 'to live is to change', and mixed in with this continuity, we experience innovation, growth, development, new directions, new births. The purpose of appropriating our personal faith history is to be aware of how God has dealt with us and to enable us to see the possibilities for growth, creativity, new directions in response to God in the present.

Telling and reflecting on our faith story also helps discernment in another way. It is a process of gradually coming into possession of our true selves, of who we truly are in relation to God. It involves accepting the light and the dark in ourselves, the strong and the weak, the godly and the sinful, the wounded and the healthy. Taking possession of ourselves, by telling, retelling and reflecting on the history of God's dealings with us, helps to set us on the road to freedom. True freedom is the ability to become the person God destined me to be; the capacity to allow my relationship with God – and hence the grace of God – to determine the shape and direction of my life. The more we take possession of our real and deepest selves through acknowledging, appropriating and accepting our personal and communal history in relation to God, the more we are able to grow in freedom. And the more we live in freedom, the more capable we are of hearing the voice of the Spirit and following where it leads.

THE SETTING OF DISCERNMENT: IMAGES OF GOD

Discernment means making choices within the context of a living relationship and continuing dialogue with God. We carry about with us our own personal images of God. They too, like the values by which we live, are the product of personal experience, education, the traditions of society, culture and church, and so on. These images, however, are not necessarily conscious. We may not be aware with our conscious minds of who God is for us and what kind of God we relate to in practice. None the less, such 'pictures' of God, hidden though they may be for much of the time, have a powerful effect on our lives: they indicate, for example, what we really think of God; they also influence how we respond to God in prayer and in life, and how we deal with other people. Just as our spontaneous dealings with others reveal our often unconscious attitudes and feelings towards them, so our words and actions – and prayer in particular – also reveal our fundamental attitudes and feelings towards God.

Turning again to discernment, it is important to recognize that our images of God, whether we are aware of them or not, are part of the framework within which we make our choices, and that they do in fact have a powerful influence on them. Discernment means allowing our ideas about who and what God is to have a hand in shaping our decisions and, through them, our lives as a whole. These images, being part of the equipment with which we choose one option or another, can have either a positive or a negative influence on that process. Some of them in fact make fruitful discernment quite difficult. Let us suppose, for example, that the dominant picture of God in my life is that of an all-powerful king who is for the most part remote, unpredictable and arbitrary in the way that he uses his power. If my life is greatly under the influence of this God, any fruitful discernment will be extremely difficult. One of the basic conditions for discernment is trust in a God who is faithful to his covenant and his promises. But this particular way of thinking about God, which incidentally is by no means uncommon, inspires fear rather than trust. I cannot with any confidence entrust myself to a God whom I perceive as being both extremely powerful and wholly unpredictable.

Discernment ultimately does mean placing ourselves as unreservedly as possible in God's hands, asking God to shape our lives through our decisions and thus allowing God to bring to fulfilment the creative work that God has already begun in us. For fruitful discernment, therefore, we need a God to whom we can entrust ourselves with confidence. Among the many Christian concepts of God that exist, those which portray God as a God of unfailing love, compassion and forgiveness are the ones most likely to offer this secure foundation.

Discernment involves making choices within a setting of prayer, of a continuing dialogue with God. It is fruitful when it is based on a right understanding of God and of ourselves in relation to God. Prayer and contemplation make us aware of who God is and who we truly are. In the presence of God we become aware of both the glory and the fragility of our condition as God's creatures. Our greatness and glory stem from the fact that we are God's children, sisters and brothers of Jesus Christ, created, chosen and made holy by God. At the same time we are conscious of being fragile and needy, and we both long for and rejoice in a God who accepts with compassion our fragility and appreciates our neediness. The Christian images of a God of unfailing, unconditional love fulfil our need for a God whom, in worshipping, we can also trust. God incarnate in Jesus Christ approaches us as one who accepts our creatureliness, our fragility; more than that, as a God who is unreservedly committed to us, who stands alongside us in the glory and the fragility of our humanity, and thus anticipates and satisfies our need for a God of compassion. Through contemplation, moreover, we become increasingly sensitive to the presence of sin, injustice, lack of love, both in ourselves and in the world around us. We recognize that we need to be in contact with a God who readily forgives, from whom liberation and salvation come as sheer undeserved gift. Thus the image of God who is revealed to us in the scriptures and most especially in the life, death and resurrection of Jesus offers a trustworthy foundation and framework for fruitful discernment.

Discernment also presupposes that this God whose love is unfailing is also continuously present and active in the world. We sometimes make the mistake of assuming, however, that this presence of God is to be found only in people, events, places, times or symbols that are explicitly and unambiguously 'sacred' or 'religious' in a conventional sense; that God is present only, for example, in saintly people, in sacraments and worship, in symbols with an unambiguously religious content, in churches and shrines or in times of prayer and felt closeness to God. Sometimes, too, we limit this presence of God to such things as these which are specifically Christian. If, however, discernment means tuning in to the action of God in the world and allowing God to shape us, then we have to have a broader vision. We have to be aware that always and everywhere, in adversity no less than in prosperity, God is creatively at work in the world to establish the reign of God, which embraces the whole world and all it contains. Discernment has to do with recognizing in the world as we experience it, on the one hand, the presence and action of God and, on the other hand, those forces and structures, in ourselves and in the world at large, which are opposed to God and which tend to destroy the reign of God.

Christian discernment also takes place within the setting of an awareness that we are the recipients of a gracious invitation from God. God's desire is to establish the reign or kingdom of God for the well-being of the whole world. For this purpose God invites us into partnership with God and with one another: each of us in our own way is invited to play a part in witnessing to the good news of the reign of God and taking part in the struggle to make God's reign a living reality. This invitation, therefore, is also part of the context within which we practise discernment. We shape our lives by the large or small choices that we make in response to it. The Christian art of discernment allows us to look at the options that lie open to us within our own circumstances and to distinguish between those choices which express acceptance of God's invitation and those which run counter to it. In all of this, moreover, God is not simply an ultimate goal, a destination we hope to reach at the end of a long, lonely road. God is rather the 'home' from which we start, the source of all life and strength, and our constant companion on the journey.

In Christian discernment, however, it is important to keep in view another fact about God which scripture and our experience repeatedly confirm: 'My ways are not your ways, nor are my thoughts your thoughts' (Isa. 55:8). Try as we may, we cannot control God. God has a way of being always ahead of us, and of turning our ordinary thoughts, ideas, plans and values upside down. God 'pulls down the mighty from their thrones and raises the lowly' (Luke 1:52). This is the God of surprises, and the story of God's dealings with us is a tale of the unexpected. If we allow God to stay close to us, God invites us constantly to open our minds and hearts more, to revise our values and our ideas about how things should be, to risk feeling insecure. God consistently takes us beyond what we thought was safe and established to something new, different and greater. In our practice of discernment it is vital that we keep in mind this quality of God's dealings with us. The impulse behind discernment is the desire to respond in love and trust to God's love. But God's wisdom sometimes looks like folly, and true discernment means being ready to be led beyond ordinary prudence and common sense into the unexpected, the unconventional, God's foolish wisdom.

CONCLUSION

So far in this book we have looked at why discernment is a necessary gift for living Christian discipleship in the church at present; we have discussed in general terms what discernment is; and we have taken a glance at those global, social, cultural, ecclesial and religious factors which make up the constant setting in which we make Christian choices. Now we turn to a closer examination of the process of discernment itself.

3

What is discernment?

'Discernment' is a popular and even over-used word in some Christian circles at the present time, and there is a danger here, as always, that over-use of a word makes its meaning so elastic as to be misleading. What this book describes as Christian discernment is not just any process of decision-making that takes place in a vaguely prayerful setting. Pausing for a few minutes of prayer at the start of a meeting and then getting down to business in the usual way is not what I would understand by Christian discernment. Nor is it merely, as is sometimes claimed, an elaborate process by which people who mean well but tend to dither about choices reach a decision, when exactly the same decision could be made more quickly and easily by 'simple common sense' or intuition. Good discernment tends to reach different conclusions from those of everyday common sense. And that is because it has to do with allowing our deepest attitudes, aspirations, values and relationships to come to the surface, so that it is they which give shape and direction to our choices. It can (and, I think, should) lead us to question and, where appropriate, change the usual assumptions, criteria and processes by which our decisions or the normal business of our meetings are governed. Moreover, it may also mean acknowledging and setting aside the masks and manipulative tactics with which we often deal with each other for our own advantage. So, having discussed in the previous two chapters the general setting in which we make Christian choices, we are now in a position to give closer attention to the question of what

Christian discernment is, and some biblical reflections will lay the foundation for that.

SOME BIBLICAL INSIGHTS

A comprehensive study of discernment in the Bible would be a whole book in itself. My aim in this section is the far more modest one of introducing a few biblical texts and images which serve to highlight different facets of the practice of discernment.

1. 'Choose life.' In the book of Deuteronomy, Moses is described as addressing the assembled people of Israel on three separate occasions about the terms of their covenant with God. In his last address to the people Moses is depicted as saying:

> See, today I set before you life and prosperity, death and disaster . . . if you love Yahweh your God and follow his ways . . . you will live and increase . . . But if your heart strays . . . you will most certainly perish . . . I set before you life or death, blessing or curse. Choose life, then, so that you and your descendants may live in the love of Yahweh your God . . . for in this your life consists (Deut. 30: 15–20).

That brings us close to the heart of what discernment is. Its overall context is a covenant with God: an agreement by which God and God's people agree to live in mutual love and fidelity. Everyday life poses a continuous succession of choices between two paths, the one leading to fulness of life in the love of God; the other leading in a direction that is ultimately dehumanizing and destructive. Discernment is the capacity in the changing circumstances of daily life to distinguish between these two paths, these two modes of living, and to 'choose life, so that you and your descendants may live in the love of Yahweh your God'. Discernment is the capacity to live a fully and truly human life.

2. *'Hear the word of the Lord.'* The metaphor of the word of the Lord also expresses what discernment essentially is. 'The word of the Lord came to me, saying . . .' is a favoured image among many of the biblical prophets. The word of God is creative, energetic, enlightening, fruitful, lifegiving (Isa. 55:10–11). The prophet's gift and task is to 'have a disciple's ear' (Isa. 50:4–5) to receive the word of the Lord in whatever context God chooses to speak; to distinguish between the genuine word of God and what cleverly but deceitfully masquerades as God's word; to read the circumstances of everyday life through the lens of God's word; to act upon the word and to recall the people to fidelity to it. To be unable or unwilling to receive the word of the Lord is to deprive oneself of the source of life, goodness, wisdom and creativity. Moreover the genuine prophet hears the word of the Lord not only in the scriptures but also in the events of history, the 'signs of the times'. Discernment, then, is the ability both to allow one's own life to be formed and guided by the word of God and to play an appropriate part in ensuring that this word also guides the life and shapes the structures of the community.

3. *Wisdom.* Obviously here we do not have the space to explore in all its complexity the image of wisdom in the Jewish scriptures. Several facets of that image, however, help us to see more clearly the richness of what is involved in discernment.

In one of the biblical traditions wisdom is personified as a woman. She is a heavenly being (Prov. 8:22–31), the feminine face of God, the first of God's creation, born 'before earth came into being' (8:22). She was present as a 'master craftsman' when God created the world and took part in setting order into creation (8:27–31), 'delighting God day after day, ever at play in his presence'. In another description she is 'a breath of the power of God, pure emanation of the glory of the almighty . . . She is a reflection of the eternal light, untarnished mirror of God's active power, image of his goodness' (Wisd. 7:25–26). She sums up, then, all that is desirable: all the potential for beauty, creativity, abundance, the unity and right ordering of the world and of human life, that belongs in the first place to God.

In another passage in Proverbs this female figure of wisdom addresses God's people, offering herself to them as God's gift and promising untold riches to anyone who accepts: 'for the man who finds me finds life'. In other parts of the wisdom books, too, wisdom is a woman who, at the city gates or at the crossroads, wherever people walk or gather, recommends them to receive and accept the beauty and riches of wisdom (Prov. 8–9, Wisd. 6:12–21). It is no surprise then that this beautiful feminine figure evokes the language of love and marriage. Solomon announces: 'She it was I loved and searched for from my youth; I resolved to have her as my bride, I fell in love with her beauty', and 'I therefore determined to take her to share my life, knowing she would be my counsellor in prosperity, my comfort in cares and sorrow' (Wisd. 8:2,9).

These and other descriptions of wisdom that are found in the wisdom literature of the Jewish scriptures include everything that I mean by the word 'discernment' in this book. This wisdom has many dimensions. Fundamentally, it is the gift of knowing the ways of God and of being able to mirror those ways in one's own conduct. It means the practical art of living in right relation to God in one's personal life and helping to order and structure the life of the community in accordance with God's designs and desires. It includes the capacity to distinguish in one's judgements and choices what is good and creative from what is evil and destructive. Those who have this gift of wisdom can eschew folly and seek the good in every circumstance. And underlying all this, there is the conviction that to have this wisdom is to share in God's own wisdom which sustains and orders aright the universe and all that it contains.

These two metaphors, the word of God and wisdom, are taken up again, of course, in the New Testament. The gospel saying, 'Blessed are those who hear the word of God and keep it' (Luke 11:28) is in a direct line with those sayings of the prophets which invoke 'the word of the Lord'. And in the prologue to the Fourth Gospel, the *logos* or Word, who was with God in the beginning, through whom all things were made and who became flesh and dwelt among us (John

1:1–18), presents the life, death and resurrection of Jesus as a new revelation of the wisdom of God. As a consequence, in a Christian as distinct from a Jewish context, because Jesus is seen as the new and privileged embodiment of God's word and God's wisdom, his Spirit informs Christian processes of decision-making and he becomes the principal norm in discernment.

4. The reign of God. The New Testament image of the reign (or kingdom) of God, characteristic of the synoptic gospels, can also help us to see what Christian discernment is. The kingdom of God is not a territorial image, and that is one reason why many people prefer to speak of the 'reign' rather than the 'kingdom' of God. Fundamentally, the reign of God means a way of living, both communally and individually, in which we allow God to be at the centre, so that 'God reigns' in every dimension of life. To be in the kingdom of God, then, means having confidence in God's love; being open to God's initiatives; looking to God to guide and lead us in our choices and actions; allowing our lives, as members of society and church and as individuals, to become increasingly a response in love to the love that God has shown to us. Living in the reign of God means doing what we can to make 'Thy will be done' a daily reality.

It would be a mistake to imagine that this reign of God is a purely individual matter. If we were to allow God truly to reign in every dimension of life, we would be concerned that not only our own attitudes, words, actions and personal relationships, but also our social structures, systems and institutions reflected the love and justice of God. If this happened, God could be said to reign both in our personal lives and in the structures and institutions by which we live in community and solidarity with each other. Discernment is one of the gifts which enables God's reign to be not only a dream but also a daily reality.

5. Paul. Earlier in this chapter we saw that in the setting of Christian discernment the incarnation, life, death and resurrection of Jesus have a crucial part to play. There is a sense

38

in which Jesus is the guide and norm in Christian choices. This leads us naturally to a consideration of Paul's understanding of the place of Jesus in the Christian life. But preparatory to that, we must look at Paul's picture of the human person.

Above all else, Paul sees the human person as a unity; but a unity with several different dimensions. For our present discussion, it is important to see that for Paul, this one person is constituted by two principles or dimensions which are ultimately in opposition to each other and inextricably combined in each of us. He calls these 'spirit' and 'flesh'. In this sense 'spirit' is the whole human person in so far as that person is open to God, capable of living in union with God's spirit and of allowing God's values to guide his or her life. 'Flesh', on the other hand, may be described as the entire human person in weakness, capable of being drawn away from God or of rebelling against God, liable to set up and worship idols and attracted by values which are abhorrent to God. As spirit we have the capacity to be transformed into a 'new creation', re-created as the creatures God desires us to be. As flesh, on the other hand, we are drawn away from the destiny God desires for us and prone to being trapped in the narrow confines of a false self and of sin. For Paul, then, each individual human person is at one and the same time both 'spirit' and 'flesh', a creature both of glory and of potentially disastrous weakness.

As Christians, therefore, we have a choice in everyday life between two paths. One option is to live 'according to the flesh', and in the letter to the Galatians Paul lists the qualities that are characteristic of such a life (Gal. 5:19). The other option is to allow ourselves to be 'led by the Spirit' (Gal. 5:18; see also Rom. 8). The qualities of this life in the Spirit are the direct opposite of those which belong to life 'according to the flesh': 'What the Spirit brings is very different: love, joy, peace, patience, kindness, goodness, trustfulness, gentleness and self-control' (Gal. 5:22). What we need therefore is the ability to distinguish in everyday life, among all the contradictory desires and attractions that we experience, what belongs to 'life according to the Spirit' from what belongs to 'life according to the flesh' and to choose accordingly. And that is the gift of discernment.

Let us take this a stage further and see how the person of Christ has a central place in this 'discernment'. Writing to the Christians in Rome, Corinth, Ephesus and other places, Paul often takes great trouble to spell out for them in some detail how they should behave as disciples of Jesus who have been introduced to life according to the Spirit. What is important in those passages for our present discussion is not so much their content as the process of reflection that they reveal: the understanding they give us of the workings of Paul's 'discernment'. In these moral exhortations Paul, as is well known, rarely quotes the actual teaching of Jesus himself to show how his followers should conduct themselves. It is not that Jesus' teaching is unimportant, but Paul approaches the question by another route.

In his own mind he sets, side by side as it were, two things: on the one hand, the current situation in Rome, Corinth, Ephesus, Philippi or wherever it may be; and on the other hand the incarnation, life, death and resurrection of Jesus. He examines these two points of focus together side by side. By reflecting on the two in reference to each other, he brings to light harmonies and discords, likenesses and contradictions between the Christians' behaviour and the meaning inherent in the life, death and resurrection of Jesus (e.g. Rom. 5–7; 1 Cor. 1–2; 8; 11; 2 Cor. 8–9; Gal. 2–5; Eph. 1–2; 5–6; Phil. 2–3; Col. 1–3; Tit. 2:11–15). In this process of reflection, the incarnation, life, death and resurrection of Jesus have a double effect. They highlight what in Rome or Corinth and in the Christians' conduct there belongs to 'the flesh' and is therefore destructive; and on the other hand they point to what are or should be the true attitudes, dispositions and conduct of the Christians to whom he is writing in the particular circumstances in which they live. For Paul, therefore, the 'mystery of Christ' acts as a key to unlock the door upon what true discipleship means for a particular group of people in a particular social, political and religious setting. Or, to change the metaphor, the whole mystery of Christ is a lens which enables Paul (and his fellow Christians) to distinguish more clearly what in their own circumstances belongs to life in the spirit from what belongs to life in the flesh, and to allow themselves to be led by the Spirit. In this process, Paul and his fellow Christians 'put on the mind of Christ' (Phil. 2:5–11).

There is another step to take before we leave Paul. Within this process of discernment, what we call the paschal mystery of the cross and resurrection of Jesus holds a special place for Paul. It brings us to the central, paradoxical mystery of the Christian faith. The cross is the sign of contradiction: it is the 'folly of God' and at the same time a revelation of God's 'wisdom', God's wise design 'hidden for generations and centuries and now revealed' (cf. Rom. 16:25; Col. 1:26). In Paul's reflections, therefore, the cross as a supreme act of God's love, becomes also the real touchstone of genuine discipleship. If the lives of Jesus' followers in some way mirror the cross of Jesus, they are true disciples. Conversely, the cross of Jesus above all else points the way to the true path of Christian discipleship.

Paul's method of reflection here sets out the basic pattern of Christian discernment. We need the dual focus: to give attention both to our own world and personal circumstances on the one hand and to the mystery of the incarnation, life, death and resurrection of Jesus on the other. The whole mystery of Christ, summed up in the folly of the cross and resurrection of Jesus, also offers us the gift of God's wisdom, a way of seeing what for us in our own circumstances is the path of true Christian discipleship.

This small collection of biblical images and insights is only a fraction of what scripture has to offer on the subject of discernment. We have not mentioned, let alone explored, other relevant biblical images and texts, such as symbols of light and darkness in the Johannine writings; what the gospels have to say about Jesus' own practice of discernment in living out his mission; the meaning of 'testing the spirits' in the letters of John, and interpretations of 'what the Spirit is saying to the churches' in the book of Revelation. Our discussion is enough, however, to provide us with a starting point for a sketch of the elements of Christian discernment.

CHOICES

Our choices are our responses to what life offers to us: taking this, accepting that; letting go of this, holding on to that; doing this rather than that; omitting or refusing to do one thing in favour of a better option. It is our choices, too, that shape our lives, and that shape reflects the kind of options we have chosen within the limits of the circumstances in which we are placed.

Choices are on a sliding scale of seriousness and it goes without saying that some have greater weight than others. At one end of the scale are the more trivial decisions which we make almost automatically, without thinking, in day-to-day living. For healthy people in an affluent society, the option of whether to have cereal for breakfast or not is a relatively trivial affair. Some everyday issues, however, do have greater importance: questions about how I treat my colleagues at work, whether to make sure the children come home early from the disco or how much time I spend with my community, can have consequences for ourselves and others that are far-reaching and far from trivial.

At the very serious end of the choices spectrum stand those decisions which are significant for us in that they represent truly crucial moments, turning points as a result of which our lives take a new shape and direction, are 'changed utterly'. It is as though at the moment of making this kind of option we gather our whole lives in our hands and, for better or worse, give them a new shape. These more crucial moments may have to do with a job, a career, a vocation, a lifestyle; a decision to marry or not to marry a particular person; a choice of celibacy; a decision to seek a divorce; a decision to ask for baptism in the church; a decision to return to the church, and so on. Most of us probably make only a few of these choices in the course of a lifetime, and spend a certain amount of time and energy running away from making them.

42

Christian discernment is often taken to mean only those processes of careful, prayerful deliberation which we undertake when faced with a particularly important decision: 'We are at a critical point but we feel that we have really discerned the next step in our life together.' 'Discernment really helped me to decide about what to do with my life.' 'We were faced with a decision about the future of St Mary's school, so we did a discernment.' 'I felt I needed a change of ministry, a change of direction, so I went through a process of discernment.'

Christian discernment as I understand it, however, is not confined to these important moments alone. It has to do with acting in the power of the Spirit as sons and daughters of the Father and brothers and sisters of Jesus Christ. This relationship with God, Father, Son and Spirit, is the context in which as disciples of Jesus we live day by day. It is not a separate compartment of daily life, but on the contrary, the ground on which everything else stands; the fundamental relationship which roots and feeds and gives shape to life as a whole and all that it contains. Christian discernment, therefore, means living in such a way that this basic fact, that we are daughters and sons of the Father and sisters and brothers of Jesus Christ, actually does shape and colour and govern all our decisions, both small and great.

Obviously, the degree of influence that a living commitment to Christian discipleship has upon our choices varies according to their level of seriousness. A living relationship with God makes little difference to what I choose to eat for lunch; it does, however, make a much greater difference to how I treat my family and my colleagues or whether I eat or drink to excess. Discernment obviously does not mean treating all decisions with equal seriousness. Part of the art, in fact, consists in learning to sift true from false values and to make sure that molehills do not become mountains, nor mountains molehills. If I am trying to live in the Spirit as a son or daughter of the Father and brother or sister of Jesus Christ, as I consciously recognize and accept these fundamental relationships, they begin to have an effect on me from within, so that even my spontaneous decisions are progressively shaped by them. For those who are in touch with God day by day, the music within shapes the whole dance.

A daily, living relationship with God, therefore, is a precondition for good discernment. To attempt to 'do discernment' in a vacuum, as it were, by simply following a set of instructions without the foundation of this living relationship with God is a misunderstanding of what discernment is and an impossible task. It is not a mental and practical process or system which, like a DIY manual or a book of recipes, can be taken out and used on any suitable occasion when a very important decision has to be made. This would make discernment into something automatic or mechanical, which it is not. Christian discernment, particularly as regards important decisions that need careful deliberation, certainly involves a process, but it is not the kind of process which, provided we follow the guidelines correctly, will automatically yield the 'right' decision in any kind of context. A process of discernment about an important choice requires the support of a form of daily living in which we are open and sensitive to the movements and leading of the Spirit of God in the path of the gospel. Fidelity to the Spirit in the daily round is the necessary soil in which large, important decisions come to fruition.

THE ELEMENTS OF DISCERNMENT

This section of the chapter will simply describe in a summary form the different elements of Christian discernment. This is intended as a preliminary outline whose details will be more fully explored in subsequent chapters.

The general context

In the first two chapters of this book we examined, from two different perspectives, the general present-day context, global, socio-cultural, ecclesial, religious, personal, in which all our discernment takes place. There is continuous interaction and

44

mutual influence between our choices and this wider context in which we live.

Moreover, it is clear from the earlier sections of this chapter that there are two main settings in which discernment has a place: namely, the circumstances of everyday life and on the other hand those occasions in which we are faced with a major decision that gives a new shape and direction to the future. Discernment in everyday life is a matter of regular reflection on daily events, within a framework of prayer, in order to see where the Spirit is leading and to follow that lead. Discernment with respect to a major decision is often a more prolonged and carefully structured process, proportionate to the seriousness of the decision itself. In each case, however, the main elements of discernment are the same. Continuing discernment in everyday life, as I have said before, is a necessary foundation and support for discernment about major choices. If I have not practised dancing in everyday life, I am liable to fall over on the big occasion.

The more immediate context

The foundation of discernment in the present is recognition and awareness of the presence and action of a loving God in the past; that is, both in our personal histories and in the history of the faith community to which we belong. (See chapter 2.)

Discernment also involves the practice of becoming aware of God as a day-to-day presence in our experience, not only in the past but also in the present. This means recognizing the presence and action of God both in the world at large, and in the smaller, interlocking personal worlds which each of us inhabits. It also entails regular prayerful reflection upon such questions as, 'Where have I met God today/this week/this last month?' 'Where is God meeting me and drawing me, in the events of my life and in the world around me?' 'Where do I feel drawn away or cut off from God in these circumstances?'

An attitude of trust and a measure of effective freedom,

therefore, are also necessary for good discernment: trust that by this means a gracious God can and will lead us to right choices; and sufficient freedom both to consider the options available in openness and honesty and to accept the outcome, whatever it may be.

The components of the process

My aim here is not to give a step-by-step description of a particular process of discernment but rather to indicate briefly the essential components of such a process.

1. Assiduous prayer. The climate or atmosphere necessary for good discernment is regular and serious prayer in which those involved in the process attempt to listen to the voice of the Spirit speaking in revelation and in the circumstances in which they are placed.

2. Adequate information. For any form of decision-making it is imperative to have sufficient information about matters which are relevant to the choices available.

3. Reflection on affective responses in relation to God. This process involves noting, interpreting and reflecting on the feelings and desires that we experience, particularly in direct or indirect response to the revelation of God. (See chapter 4.)

4. Weighing the reasons. Being adequately informed about the circumstances surrounding each of the options available allows us to give due weight to the reasons for and against each option, which is also an essential part of the discernment process. (See chapter 6.)

5. Confirmation. It is also to be expected that, once a decision has been made, we will experience in some form either confirmation of the decision or its opposite, unease or a sense of a need for further searching.

Christian discernment, therefore, whether in the course of daily living or in the context of a major decision, is a question of sifting through a number of different matters in turn: the circumstances and options about which choices are to be made; our feelings and thoughts about these circumstances and options within a framework of prayer and awareness of God; the revelation of God, especially as given in the life, death and resurrection of Jesus. In this process we gradually become aware of harmonies or disharmonies between the mystery of Christ and our own lives and this awareness offers a guide and norm for the choices we make.

DISCERNMENT AND THE WILL OF GOD

It is often said that discernment is concerned with finding the will of God in the circumstances of daily life and with regard to our major choices. And that is correct. At the same time it is important to understand what we really mean by 'the will of God', what picture it evokes in our minds, because sometimes we seem to interpret it in ways which can be misleading and arouse expectations that can never in fact be met.

One kind of model or way of thinking of the will of God seems to offer a picture that, from the point of view of discernment, is less than helpful. It is as though the whole universe and the whole of human history, past, present and to come, are like an infinitely intricate and unimaginably sophisticated play. God has written the script of the play beforehand and is its director; our task is to find out what part has been assigned to us, learn the script and perform it under God's more or less minutely detailed direction. According to this image of what God's will is, discernment is seen as a means of finding the role into which God has placed us, fitting neatly into this role and giving the performance of our lives.

One of the main strengths of this image is that, when people believe that they have in fact found their assigned place in God's great drama, the knowledge brings with it a sense of security, of having 'found the right place'. There are, however, several reasons why this is not a helpful or satisfactory way of understanding the will of God. Principally, it is a very

47

restrictive way of thinking about human freedom. It tends to present life as a task to be performed in a particular way, rather than as a gratuitous gift, and it limits our freedom, arguably the most precious of human gifts, to no more than fitting dutifully into a role assigned to us by God, and being obedient in every detail to God's direction. Moreover, this 'play' image, whether we believe in it explicitly or it is one of those unconscious images that childhood or education has instilled into us, can also be a source of great anxiety, because of the false expectations it raises. It may happen that we take part in a process of discernment with the perhaps unconscious expectation that somehow in the course of it 'where God wants us to be now' in the great play will be revealed to us. 'Is my role in God's play to stay in St Luke's Catholic school or to apply for a job at Brixton High?' When this hoped-for revelation does not in fact take place, anxiety, confusion, dejection or disillusionment with the whole idea of discernment can ensue. And after a great expense of anxious effort we still may not know 'what God wants'.

The God revealed to us in scripture, however, is not like a pernickety and overbearing director of a play who wants to determine every gesture and movement of the company, nor like a tyrant who imposes his will on his subjects whether they like it or not. God deals with us more like parents with their daughters and sons, or friends with those whom they love: God has hopes and desires for the world and for us and provides whatever is necessary to allow them to be fulfilled. Our true destiny and happiness lie in helping to create the kind of world that offers a framework within which all can have the life and the destiny which God desires for them.

In a context of discernment, therefore, it is more helpful to speak of God's hopes and desires for us rather than of God's will, which can appear to be harsh and restricting instead of liberating. This is not the place to try to describe the content of God's hopes and desires, but they have been revealed to us in various ways. If we have eyes to see, we can perceive them in creation, in life as it unfolds in us and around us and in the gifts that each of us receives from God. Moreover, the word of God is another place in which God's hopes and desires become clear to us. Specifically, the life, teaching, death and resurrection of Jesus sum up what it means to be truly human, what God in love hopes we will become.

The key to finding the will of God lies in our use of the gift of freedom. In the context of discernment, it is important to recall that God, far from imposing on us the fulfilment of his hopes and desires, graciously invites us to collaborate with God and with one another to bring them about. Our true freedom lies in our capacity to respond to this invitation: to cooperate with God in creating a world that enables us, individually and collectively, to become both now and in the future the people that God desires us to be. Discernment, therefore, is more than a pragmatically effective way of making choices. It is rather a framework which enables us to join in partnership with God in making choices which will help to bring about the fulfilment of God's generous hopes and desires for the world and for us.

Perhaps music and dance, then, offer an illuminating image of what it means to 'discern God's will'. We hear the Spirit's music in creation, in our own gifts, in life as it unfolds in us and in the world around us, and in the word of God. God's gracious invitation is that we dance to that music. Jesus, as the song says, is the 'Lord of the Dance'. True freedom and discernment mean that, while keeping our eyes on him, we create, not in isolation but together, our own gestures and movements in tune with the Spirit's music. Those who really listen to the music have the freedom to invent their own steps and movements and then they find that in fact they are all dancing in unison.

FELLOW PILGRIMS

Discernment is clearly one setting in which the presence and help of a skilled and trusted 'fellow pilgrim', 'soul friend' or spiritual guide is extremely helpful. The principal role of such a person is to accompany a fellow Christian on a journey of faith and, in doing so, to enable him or her to discover the leading of the Spirit in the circumstances of life. This primarily involves helping and enabling the other person to practise discernment and thus to grow in the life of Christian discipleship.[1]

1 For an introduction to spiritual guidance, see, among many others, *Soul Friend* by Kenneth Leech (Sheldon Press, London 1977); and *The Practice of Spiritual Direction* by William A. Barry and William J. Connolly (Seabury Press, New York 1983).

4

Consolation and desolation

The previous chapter stated that, within the framework of prayer as a continuing dialogue with God, discernment involves us in a twofold process of reflection. One aspect of this reflection is the consideration and interpretation of our *affective* responses to God and to the world; the other is a matter of weighing carefully all the *reasons* or *arguments* for and against each of the options with which we are faced when choices have to be made. This present chapter and the next will explore the first part of this process, and chapter 6 will look more fully at the second.

AFFECTIVITY AND REASON

We have already had reason to emphasize, when discussing St Paul, that the human person is fundamentally a unity; a complex, multi-dimensional unity, no doubt, composed of many qualities and relationships with the external world, but still basically one single whole. Within that unity, of course, we can distinguish different aspects or dimensions, and at this present stage of our discussion of discernment we are concerned with two of those dimensions in particular: affectivity and reason. It is helpful to think of our affective life, not as a separate part of us, but as the whole human person in so far as he or she is engaged in responding with feeling, desire and will to the world and to God. On the other hand, reason is the whole human person in so far as he or she is engaged in understanding, reasoning, analysing, distinguishing, making judgements or evaluating – everything that we associate with the activity of the mind.

Obviously, it would be a mistake to imagine that these two dimensions of our existence operate in independence from each other. On the contrary, being two aspects of the one person – or the one person seen from two different perspectives – they interpenetrate each other and are in constant interaction. Our feelings and desires are stirred by what we understand, know, reason about and evaluate. It may be a person (including ourselves), a situation in which we are involved, an option or choice that lies before us, an aspect of our own inner lives, and so on. Alternatively, the 'object' that arouses our feelings may be God as revealed to us or something wholly imaginary. Whatever the 'object', it is something known at least minimally. And just as our feelings are evoked by what we know and think, so also what we feel is capable in its turn of affecting, both positively and negatively, what we think, know and judge about ourselves, the world around us and God. Lovers are notoriously blind, and judges often counsel juries not to let their feelings sway their judgements. There is constant mutual interaction, therefore, between the affective life and the life of the mind. Moreover, this interaction by no means rules out the possibility of conflict between these two dimensions. Lack of harmony between 'heart' and 'head' is a common experience, and in fact is often a necessary stage in fruitful discernment and growth towards wholeness.

Any balanced process of discernment necessarily takes account of both the rational and the affective aspects of our existence. If, on the one hand, we suppress our feelings and take no notice of them, we run the risk of losing our way in cold rationality, of living solely 'in the head'. On the other hand, if we exclude the voice of reason, we are in danger of being entirely governed by swings of moods or waves of emotion and desire. 'Use your head and trust your feelings', the title of a recent discussion of discernment, neatly sums up the balance and interaction which are necessary for good discernment.[1]

This general introduction now leads us naturally into the next phase of our discussion, which is to explore more fully the process of reflecting on our affective life that discernment involves. We will consider this process in three main stages, understanding also, of course, that the whole process of discernment takes place within a framework of prayer and a living relationship with God.

I. BEING AWARE OF FEELINGS, MOODS, DESIRES

The first step in dealing with our feelings in discernment, whether in the daily events of ordinary life or with regard to a major decision, is to be aware of and to note what we feel in connection with the circumstances and choices that concern us.

It is obvious that some feelings are more significant than others, and in ordinary speech we talk of some as being 'deeper' than others. Some of our desires, moods and feelings are very transient or superficial; they pass quickly and do not make any noticeable difference to how we act and live. We may feel pleased or shed a few tears, but the feelings which cause these reactions make no substantial difference to our choices or our actions. We do, however, have moods, desires, attractions, needs and other affective experiences which make a significant difference to how we act and how we live. There is a level of feeling which does affect, either positively or negatively, the choices we make. These deeper feelings provide the energy and drive necessary for important decisions and effective action. Love, anger, a mood of confidence, a sense of discouragement, a passion for justice, a thirst for God, all these and many others move us to choose and to act and thus give a particular colour, shape and direction to our lives. It is these deeper, more significant feelings that have a part to play in discernment.

The moods, desires and other feelings that are especially important in discernment are those that have to do with God, God's dealings with the world as a whole, and with us as individuals. But while obviously 'sacred' things do often serve to evoke and focus our feelings and desires towards God, they are not the only settings in which we can experience a wide

53

range of different moods, feelings and desires which are more or less explicitly associated with God and with God's dealings with us. For many Christians, and many who would not see themselves as particularly religious, the significant events of life, it may be an illness, an accident, bereavement, marriage, the birth of a child, divorce, redundancy, unemployment or an event in the political world, can all call forth a range of different feelings towards God and the ways in which God is present and active in the world.

As we have seen, the framework within which fruitful Christian discernment takes place is one in which we explicitly acknowledge that we are called to live in the Spirit as daughters and sons of the Father and brothers and sisters of Jesus Christ. Experience shows that when this actually is the context and atmosphere within which the whole of life is contained, we become more sensitive to the presence of God in all creation and history. As a result of this, circumstances which previously we did not perhaps associate with God at all begin to speak to us of God and evoke in us in response moods and feelings of all kinds towards God and God's presence in the world.

Faced with the ordinary circumstances of life or with a major decision, we are likely to experience a wide range of different and perhaps conflicting feelings and moods, impulses and desires, which are directly or indirectly associated with God. Joy, peace, sadness, turmoil, confidence, fear, anger, resentment, jealousy, energy and enthusiasm or listlessness and lethargy, these are only some of the responses that we are likely to find in ourselves. What discernment offers here is a fuller understanding of the significance of those feelings. The first step towards that is actually to note the feelings that we experience; to answer the question: What are my feelings with regard to this particular situation or this major decision that I have to make? And it is especially important to give careful attention to those feelings which are aroused in us within a setting of prayerful meditation, because that is a context in which we are likely to be more susceptible than usual to the action of the Spirit and more able to allow our truest and deepest feelings to come to the surface.

II. INTERPRETING OUR FEELINGS, MOODS, DESIRES

As a help towards a fuller understanding of what we experience, the Christian tradition of discernment distinguishes between two different kinds of affective responses to God. In this book, following the practice of recent developments in the spirituality associated with Ignatius Loyola, I am using the terms '(spiritual) consolation' and '(spiritual) desolation' for these two groups of feelings. It is often pointed out that 'consolation' and 'desolation' are not wholly satisfactory terms and many people find them awkward, but to my mind they are as good as any that are available, and in any case, once we know from experience what we mean by them, the terms themselves become less important.[2] The experiences that come under these headings may be called 'spiritual', not because they exist in some area of our personal life that is 'non-material', nor because they are different in nature from the other feelings that we experience; but rather because, for the person who has them, they are associated with or evoked by God and things that have to do with God.[3] They have as their 'object' God, God's dealings with us, God's desires or will for us. Just as gazing at a Rembrandt painting evokes in us feelings of admiration and wonder not only for the painting but also for the painter, so also contemplating the world and all that it contains as the work of God can stir in us in response a wide range of affective reactions, a variety of feelings, desires and moods. These are the responses that the Ignatian tradition of discernment calls either consolation or desolation. The first term, consolation, refers to what we might ordinarily consider to be positive or creative moods, desires or feelings. The category of desolation on the other hand comprises the affective experiences that we would ordinarily see as negative or destructive.

The terms consolation and desolation, in the sense in which I am using them here, include two levels of meaning. The more immediate level, and the one more easily grasped, is that of our affective experience: the feelings, moods or desires which are elicited by our experience of life and which can easily be named – anger, resentment, envy, guilt, peace, joy, happiness, confidence, love, a longing for justice, and so on. There is, however, a second level of ourselves which is not so easily brought to the surface of our awareness. That is the more fundamental level of being: the fact of where we actually stand in relation to God; the level at which God knows us and is present in us in grace.

The practice of discernment relies much on the fact that all the different dimensions of the human person are interconnected and interact with each other. When, at the deepest level of being, we move towards God or in opposition to God, this movement has its repercussions in our affective life: our conscious feelings, moods and desires are touched. Similarly in the other direction: when our feelings are stirred by our experience of the world around us, this has its repercussions at the deeper level of how we actually stand in relation to God: we are moved towards or against God. Thus our affective movements and responses, which we can relatively easily be aware of and name, are signs of how we actually stand in relation to God, at a deeper, more hidden level of ourselves. In the waters of a lake, sounds and movement near the surface travel through the water and can be picked up at the depths. Similarly, currents, sounds and movements in the depths cause disturbances nearer the surface. Part of the art of discernment is to reflect on our conscious thoughts and feelings as indicators of where we really are in relation to God at the core of our being.

Types of consolation and desolation

Let us begin this section with four examples.

(1) Rebecca is a woman in her forties who ten years ago discovered that her husband was an alcoholic. After much wrangling, they were eventually divorced. For a long time Rebecca has felt angry with God. She used to be a regular churchgoer, but has now not been able to bring herself to enter a church for more than three years.

(2) James and Fiona are a young couple who have been

looking forward with great enthusiasm to getting married. In order to prepare for their marriage, they went to make a retreat together three months before the wedding. For the first two days of the retreat James's prayer was full of joy and peace and gratitude. On the third day he felt empty, restless, discouraged and all his fears about the future and about the commitment he and Fiona were soon to make came crowding in on him.

(3) Martha is a deacon in a busy, poor, inner-city parish. Over a period of five years she has built up a thriving ministry and the parish community has grown and matured greatly under her leadership. For the past few months, however, her whole life and ministry in the parish have seemed empty and meaningless to her, though she cannot understand why. She is seriously considering giving the whole thing up.

(4) Mick is a cheerful, happy, easy-going young bachelor. He is highly paid and claims that his one serious interest is having a good time. Recently, ever since a friend of his was killed in a car accident, he has begun to feel dissatisfied with his life from time to time, which makes him very uncomfortable indeed.

These examples illustrate several important aspects of the experiences of consolation and desolation. In (1) for instance, Rebecca's anger seems to be destructive, to create a block between herself and God and therefore to be an experience of desolation. Examples (2) and (3) illustrate circumstances in which good Christian people typically experience changes of mood and forms of desolation. We will have occasion to discuss Mick in (4) in more detail later in this chapter.

Movements or states of feeling that we in some way associate with God are experiences of either consolation or desolation. It is obviously not possible to give a list of the full range of these experiences. It might be helpful, however, to describe some typical examples of each.

Common experiences of consolation are: a sense of confidence in God and in the love of God for the world and for us; any experience which leads to a deepening and strengthening of that confidence; an appreciation of my life and all that it contains as God's gift; a sense that a person or an event in my life is a gift or an 'epiphany', a place where I meet God; an attraction to the greater good; a movement of love or desire towards God; a sense of being at peace and in harmony with God, others and ourselves; an awareness of being a sinner and of needing and receiving God's forgiveness; rejoicing in weakness in the sense in which Paul describes the experience (2 Cor. 12); an experience of inner, personal freedom or liberation; a desire and movement towards loving and serving others in the name of Jesus; a longing to be part of the struggle for the reign of God, at whatever cost to myself; a readiness to follow Jesus even to the cross; a felt knowledge of the presence of God in creation and history.

Desolation, on the other hand, is an experience of the opposite of these. Rather than opening us out to God, it seems to set a block between us and God and closes us in on ourselves in a downward spiral. It can include such experiences as: a sense that one's life is empty and meaningless; a state of self-disgust, self-hatred; a weakening or a loss of confidence in God and in God's love, with a resulting feeling of profound discouragement; a movement of love or desire which takes us away from God; a sense of being at odds with God and with oneself; a time when God seems to be absent; being trapped in a circle of remorse and guilt at one's own weakness and sinfulness; an attraction to what is less good; an inability to accept or trust in God's forgiveness; a reluctance or real unwillingness to love and serve others in the name of Christ; an aversion from whatever has to do with the reign of God; feeling revolted or fearful by the prospect of following Christ, and especially by the cross; an experience of being not-free, of being paralysed by fear, anxiety, attachments, addiction; a sense that God is absent from the world and from the events of one's life; an apparent inability to 'meet' God at all.

In this context, therefore, the terms consolation and desolation do not refer to one particular feeling such as peace, joy, anger, discouragement, confidence. They refer rather to a wide range of affective movements and states, and offer a way of distinguishing between two kinds of feeling.

It would be a mistake to think that consolation and desolation are always (or even normally) 'peak' experiences. For many people, 'peak' experiences in a religious context are comparatively rare, and some never have them at all. Though powerful inner movements which make a strong impression on us are the ones we most easily remember, if we had to rely entirely on them, discernment would be impossible because they are so rare. In times of more than usually intense prayer such as a retreat, we are more likely to be aware of higher peaks and lower troughs. The feelings that form the staple ingredients of discernment, however, are more often than not 'room temperature' experiences, moods or movements and changes of feeling that take place within the framework of our everyday dealings with life and God rather than extreme swings of feeling.

Differences between consolation and desolation

In the context of discernment, one of the central practical questions is this: How do I know that this particular experience (either my own or that of a person whose discernment I am trying to facilitate) is consolation or desolation?

The answer to that question is more complex than at first sight might appear. The complexity arises because, in terms of our relationship with God, our affective experience, taken in itself, is ambiguous. Discernment would be wonderfully easy if we could make a simple equation: consolation means pleasant and desolation means unpleasant feelings or moods – but unfortunately the truth is not so simple. To know whether the particular mood, desire or feeling of a given moment is an experience of consolation or desolation, it is not enough to look at it and reflect on it by itself, in isolation from the rest of life. On the contrary, we can grasp the true meaning, in relation to God, of our feelings, moods and desires only by looking at them within the setting of the shape and direction of our lives as a whole.

Let us take an example. An experience of 'inner peace' with regard to one of a range of options within a decision that we are making is often said to be an experience of consolation; a sign that we are in harmony with God and with ourselves in opting for this particular course of action. An experience of 'inner peace', however, is more difficult to interpret than that. A person whose heart is basically set on satisfying his or her own desires and interests without much regard for others, for the reign of God or for living the gospel, can experience a form of 'inner peace' when those fundamentally self-centred desires are being satisfied. In this case the 'inner peace' may be more akin to complacency, a sense of satisfaction with oneself, than to 'the peace which the world cannot give'. And again, if I am the kind of person who in any circumstances finds it difficult to make choices, my feeling of 'inner peace' when, after a struggle, I have chosen a particular option, *may* be no more than a sense of relief at actually having finally come to a decision at all, irrespective of whether I have chosen the better part or not. We need to look at all these experiences in a wider setting, therefore, in order to understand whether they should be described as consolation or desolation.

Two different directions

Ignatius Loyola's guidelines on discernment can help us to take this explanation further. We grasp the meaning of a particular affective experience in relation to the whole stream of life of the individual of which it is a part. In this sense the whole life of a person can be seen as moving in one of two fundamental directions, as having one of two basic orientations.

The first group of people that we need to look at are those who, for one reason or another, give little time or attention to God, the reign of God or the fulfilment of the two great commandments to love God and one's neighbour (cf. *The Spiritual Exercises*, 314)[4]. Mick, whom I briefly described earlier in this chapter, might be taken as a person of this type. Their principal and perhaps even exclusive interest is in themselves. Their overriding concern is to satisfy their own desires and needs, with little or no regard for what effect that might have on others. They have no interest in living a Christian or godly life, and if they reflect at all on the goodness or otherwise of their own behaviour, it is mainly in order to justify themselves and the way in which they live. Their main focus is self-gratification, and comfort, personal ambition, wealth or status are among their gods. Most of their energy goes into 'looking after Number One'.

Clearly that is only a sketch of a way of living, of the direction that a person's life might take, and if I have described it in a rather extreme form, it is in order to highlight a general orientation. If we try to interpret certain affective responses and moods that such a person might report, we have to take into account the direction in which her or his life in general is moving. I have said earlier that a sense of 'inner peace', of tranquillity, of confidence, a feeling of being in harmony with oneself, are ambiguous. In the case of people such as I have just described, a sense of peace or confidence would tend to confirm them in the present direction of their lives, which are neglectful of God or of any greater good than the satisfaction of their own desires and needs. In this case, from a Christian perspective, these experiences are signs of a state of opposition to God and God's desires, for they are confirming a way of life that is contrary to what God desires for us. On the other hand, experiences of inner turmoil, conflict, a feeling of inner emptiness, or a sense of meaninglessness, while certainly painful, are in fact likely to be signs of 'the sting of conscience', of the beginnings of a spiritual awakening, a subtle and perhaps slow but none the less real movement of grace.

In so far as they are drawing them towards God and the kind of life that God desires for us, therefore, such painful and challenging feelings and moods are in fact experiences of consolation in the setting of the lives of these particular people (cf. Exx 314).

The second group of people to be considered in this setting are those who honestly desire to live in the Spirit as children of the Father and brothers and sisters of Jesus and take effective steps to collaborate with God in bringing this about

(Exx 315). In this case, the terms 'consolation' and 'desolation' have their more usual meanings. Experiences of inner joy and peace, moods of confidence and encouragement in faith, a sense of being in harmony with oneself and with God, times of true creativity, and so on, are true consolation: signs of the presence of the Spirit, of growth in union of mind and heart with God and other Christians, indicators that the reign of God really is present. And conversely, times of darkness and confusion, moods of discouragement, emptiness, anxiety, meaninglessness, destructiveness, and so on, are truly experiences of desolation, signs that there is something at work in us that tends to draw us away from God and hinder the life of faith and the growth of the reign of God.

The key to knowing whether our present or past feelings, moods and desires are experiences of consolation or desolation, therefore, is to set them in the context of the general direction, in relation to God, of the life of the individual who experiences them. Experiences of peace, joy, harmony, encouragement, and so on, are signs at the level of feeling that an option, a course of action or a situation are in harmony with that general direction. On the other hand, experiences of darkness, emptiness, disharmony, and so on, are signs, at the affective level, of an inner conflict between a person's present experience and the general direction of his or her life in relation to God (cf. Exx 335).

We are now in a position to attempt a more theological description of the differences between consolation and desolation; a description, that is, in terms of God's dealings with us and our responses to God. From what we have just been discussing, it is clear that the term 'consolation' is applied to: those experiences that draw us towards God; experiences, whatever they may be, that help people to grow creatively in the life of faith, hope and love and to become what God intended them to be; experiences that open us out in generous, creative love and service of God and others; experiences that lead us to search for the reign of God; experiences that in some way or other move us to live in the Spirit as sons and daughters of the Father and sisters and brothers of Jesus. Desolation, on the other hand, is the exact contrary of this.

The name 'desolation' is given to: experiences whose direction of flow is away from or in opposition to God; experiences, whatever they may be, that impede growth in the life of faith, hope and love or make us less the people God desires us to be; those experiences that lead us to focus on ourselves and our own egotistic interests, to the exclusion of God and others; experiences that lead us away from living the gospel more fully, that move us to oppose the reign of God or hinder us from living in the Spirit as sons and daughters of the Father and sisters and brothers of Jesus (cf. Exx 316–17).

More about consolation

This allows us to introduce further nuances into our discussion.

1. 'Painful consolation'. So far, for people who are honestly seeking the reign of God, we have associated consolation with what might be called pleasant or positive feelings: encouragement, joy, peace, confidence, trustfulness, hopefulness, and so on. But it is also important to note another kind of experience which can be extremely painful but which is in fact a form of consolation. I have in mind here, for example, the feelings of shame, humiliation, sorrow or confusion aroused when we confront our own weakness, fragility, sinfulness before God and our need of reconciliation; or the sorrow, anger or fear that we feel when we look at the pain, oppression and injustice in the world around us; or the sadness and confusion evoked by contemplation of the passion and death of Jesus. Being present, in prayer, at the passion and death of Jesus might also bring to the surface memories of suffering in our own lives which remain unhealed. There is no doubt that all these and similar experiences are painful. They are, however, true consolation in so far as they are creative rather than destructive, and are moments of transformation which lead us to live more fully the life of the Spirit in the path of the gospel.

And in fact in these experiences people often report that in the midst of the pain and confusion they have a sense, however obscure, of peace, joy and serenity, like a small candle flame in a storm. Somehow they know that this affliction, painful though it undoubtedly is, is the work of the Spirit of God and a share in the paschal mystery of dying and rising to new life.

2. *'False consolation'*. 'It is a mark of the evil spirit to assume the appearance of an angel of light' (Exx 332). Earlier in this chapter I described two groups of people whose lives, in relation to God and the world around them, could be seen to be moving in opposite directions. I would like to give some attention now to certain experiences which people in the second group in particular are liable to have; especially those whose commitment to the reign of God is sincere, heartfelt and central to all that they do. At first sight these experiences appear to be times of consolation. On reflection, however, or from their consequences, they prove to be only apparently so; they are experiences of 'false' or misleading consolation. Let us have a look at some examples.

(1) Paul is a hard-working, well-disposed man in his mid-thirties. He is married to Sheila and they have three children whose ages range from three to eleven. The family are regular churchgoers, but they have had little regular contact with the church beyond that. About a year ago, however, Paul was invited to join a parish prayer group. At one of the meetings he had an experience in which he believed God was calling him to give himself more generously in his Christian commitment. Since then he has been spending more and more time working in the parish and with the local handicapped children's group. This has put a great strain on his family life. After several fierce arguments, Sheila threatens to leave him if he does not give up the prayer group and his other commitments. He gives them up but becomes discouraged and disillusioned with anything to do with religion.

(2) Jane is a forty-five-year-old single woman who was in charge of a ward in a hospice for the dying in a large city. She is a committed Christian, a prayerful person and was a

valued member of the hospice staff. She enjoyed prayer and some time ago she felt drawn increasingly to spending long periods of time in prayer. Later, she decided to leave the hospice and take up part-time agency nursing in order to be able to give more time to prayer. Eventually, against the advice of her friends, she entered a contemplative religious community, but after eighteen months there she was advised to leave. Now she feels disoriented, confused and angry with God.

(3) Anne is a committed and serious-minded religious sister in her late twenties. She has a busy life as a teacher in an inner-city secondary school, and it is work that she enjoys. Three years ago, in her annual retreat, she had a powerful experience of prayer which made a deep impression on her. As a result, she decided that she needed more prayer in her everyday life, so she added an extra hour on to her daily prayer most days of the week. By the end of the year she was very tired and realized that she had been away from school with illness more days in that year than ever before. At the same time her prayer had become difficult and dry; gradually she lost her taste for prayer and gave it up completely, apart from routinely attending community prayer.

The subtlety of these experiences is quite typical of the ways in which our inner forces of egoism and resistance to God and our capacity for self-deception can come into play. All those individuals in the examples are good people acting in good faith. It is their good qualities themselves – prayerfulness, generosity, openness, integrity – which by some kind of perversity bring them harm and lead them into paths that destroy their inner peace and turn out to be debilitating and destructive, while all the time they believed they were really in possession or in pursuit of a greater good. One of the functions of a good spiritual director or soul friend is to help an individual to guard against false consolation of this kind.

In each case the people concerned enjoy an experience of consolation in the setting of personal prayer. That experience draws them towards God and what appears to be a fuller living of the gospel. They all also make certain decisions under the influence of that experience. For different reasons, peculiar to the circumstances of each, the courses of action they undertake end in sadness and desolation. The consolation they experienced was apparently misleading. They were in pursuit of a greater good but found themselves deceptively drawn to what in the end turned out to be a lesser good.

Any instance of consolation, especially when it has a powerful impact on people and moves them to make significant changes in behaviour or lifestyle, needs careful reflection. Any individual experience of consolation, particularly if it makes a powerful impression, needs to be looked at and acted upon only in the wider context of the life of the person as a whole. That seems very obvious, but it is often forgotten. It allows excessive enthusiasm to be checked and the experience of consolation, powerful and important though it may be, to be balanced by other factors in the situation which may be equally important, though less exciting. Part of the difficulty in the three examples I have quoted is that one experience or one area of experience of the individuals concerned is interpreted in isolation from the rest of life and thus allowed to dominate both their own lives and the lives of others.

In such cases, too, the tradition and practice of Christian discernment offer another helpful reminder. It is wise to distinguish between the actual time of consolation and what might be called its 'afterglow': the psychological and emotional effects which remain, often for a long time, after the experience itself has passed. In the warmth and fervour of the afterglow we are liable to make choices which lead to desolation and are ultimately destructive for ourselves or for others.

Often we only discover the misleading effects of the experience of consolation some time after it has taken place. The advice which Ignatius Loyola gives for dealing with such instances is worth noting. Once we have discovered that we have been misled, we should trace back the chain of thoughts, feelings and choices to the point at which, we can see in retrospect, things started to go wrong. This helps both to diminish the confusion and disappointment that may have arisen, and to guard against repeating the same mistake on another occasion (Exx 333).

More about desolation

Desolation occurs when we resist the action of the Spirit of God in us. This resistance may be willed; it may be a resistance that we are aware of but apparently unable to do anything about; or it may be an unconscious resistance. Let us look at each of these possibilities in turn.

(1) Suppose Amanda is in a situation in which she has to make an important but difficult choice about which of several possible courses of action she should adopt. She approaches the decision by meditating on the gospels with the desire to follow in the Spirit the example of Jesus. In the course of her prayer and deliberations she becomes aware that, everything considered, option B would be the best choice to make in the circumstances. Here, however, she meets a difficulty. This option involves breaking a long-standing friendship. In fact, though she feels that this friendship is a source of desolation, a burden she is obliged to carry rather than a source of joy, and though she feels angry and resentful towards her friend, she cannot bring herself to break the friendship. In the end she does not choose option B and her desolation continues.

(2) Let us imagine, secondly, that Rita is in a situation in which she has to make an important choice. She feels drawn to option P, and it appears to be the one which most clearly embodies a spirit of Christian faith and love. It is also, however, the most risky, the least safe. Option Q is also a good choice, and it is also much more secure, sensible and prudent. In the course of trying to make the decision, Rita becomes aware that waves of mistrust, fear and discouragement arise in her whenever she considers option P, and they threaten to paralyse her. In this case fear and mistrust cause resistance and desolation. They are unwilled – Rita wants to overcome them – but they seem insurmountable.

(3.1) When our resistance to the work of the Spirit is something of which we are unaware, the operations of desolation are more subtle and less obvious. As a third example, let us suppose that Bill is trying to decide what to do with his life, and it is a choice between two alternatives, both of which are good. He feels drawn towards option X because he thinks that he would be happy and content in it, and that it would give him scope for sharing his life and his gifts with people whom he loves. He also feels uncertain and even guilty about it, however, because he is afraid that, in choosing it, he would be doing 'what he wants' rather than 'what God wants'. He believes that God (and other people) have very high expectations of him (though he is not aware of the extent to which this image of God in fact governs his behaviour and causes desolation). He sees another option, Y, as an extremely good course of action that would fulfil these high expectations, but it would be difficult to accomplish, he does not feel attracted to it and he is not sure that he has the right gifts for it. He is puzzled and worried, however, by the fact that he experiences confusion, a storm of conflicting feelings and a sense of heaviness and darkness of spirit when he considers the second option and he finds himself pulled now in one direction now in another.

In this case, what Bill experiences is a conflict between a sense of obligation associated with a particular image of God and a more deeply-felt attraction towards option X. He is confused by the experience of desolation because he is not aware of the lack of freedom which such a demanding image of God imposes on him.

(3.2) Suppose, as a fourth example, that Tony is a busy parish priest: conscientious, prayerful, hard-working, devoted and on the whole contented in his ministry. There are times, however, when he seems to go to pieces: he neglects his work, he stops praying, he feels an aversion towards pastoral work, he is dogged by lethargy, every small task seems an irritating chore, he becomes short-tempered, he sleeps much more than usual, but the sleep does not refresh him. The doctor says he

is healthy and not suffering from depression. At these times
he begins to think about leaving the priesthood.

In this example, the tendency of the desolation, as ever, is
to hinder the greater good: it makes Tony unhappy and
neglectful in his ministry. The source of the desolation could
be uncovered by further patient reflection or with the help of
a friend or spiritual director.

For those who are genuinely trying to live a life of faith the
experience of desolation is often very painful: an affliction
they would rather not have. From another point of view,
however, some forms of desolation can be very appealing. If
our desolation takes the form, for instance, of lethargy, lassi-
tude towards any higher good, desire for immediate self-
gratification, an attraction towards passing what is really
excessive time in entertainment and pleasure, its siren voice
can be very alluring. It speaks winningly to our sensuality,
to our love of ease, to the forces of egoism, which rarely die
altogether. When this occurs, it is not uncommon to want to
hold on to our desolation. Going along with the desolation is
far easier than making the effort either to withstand its appeal
or to move out of it. At such times, too, self-justification often
plays a strong role: we search around for reasons which will
justify remaining in desolation and making no effort against
it.

None the less, a positive rather than a negative evaluation
of desolation, in spite of its destructive potential, is characteristic of the Ignatian tradition of discernment. The logic of
this apparent paradox is simple. While desolation, as we have
just seen, arises from resistance to or neglect of the working
of the Spirit (and in that sense, of course, could be judged to
be 'negative'), it is nevertheless a sign that the Spirit is in
fact at work and an indication of where the Spirit is stimulat-
ing healing or growth. Points at which desolation occurs are
points of potential growth in the life of faith. If the Spirit
were not present, there would be no friction or resistance.
That is why Ignatius Loyola and others insist that in discernment we review and reflect upon our experiences of both
consolation and desolation. Both are signs of the presence of

the Spirit, and reflecting on both helps us to discover the direction in which the Spirit is moving, the place in which the reign of God is to be found.

III. HANDLING CONSOLATION AND DESOLATION

So far in this chapter we have been looking at a process of understanding and sifting through our affective responses to life and to God, within the framework of a living relationship with God. Now, in this last section, we will move on to a further stage and examine ways of dealing with and acting upon these responses in order to make choices and to enhance growth in the life of faith and Christian discipleship.

The basic principle here is fairly straightforward: if we wish to follow the leading of the Spirit, we should move with and build upon our experiences of consolation. Conversely, we should try to ensure that we do not act out experiences of desolation, that we withstand their influence and avoid going along in the direction in which they would move us. The logic of that is easy enough. As we have seen, 'consolation' refers to those creative affective experiences which move us towards living the gospel and the reign of God more fully, towards the fulness of life with God; while 'desolation' moves us in the opposite direction and, if acted out, has destructive consequences. 'Follow consolation' and 'oppose or withstand desolation', is therefore sound advice.

It is not so much isolated instances of consolation and desolation that are significant in discernment. Isolated movements or changes of feeling may be due to many different causes and may easily be misread. A far surer guide is the pattern of these experiences over a period of time. If I am faced with an important choice, for example, I note and reflect on how my feelings as regards my different options are consistent or change during the time in which I am considering the decision. The consistency, changes and cumulative effect of these experiences are helpful indications of where the right choice lies. Similarly in day-by-day discernment in everyday life: the patterns of continuity and change in my experiences of consolation and desolation over a period of time act as pointers to my next steps on the path of discipleship.

Acting on consolation

Earlier in this chapter we had a close look both at what is meant by consolation, and at some of the experiences of 'false consolation' that can occur. Acting on consolation means noting those times and places in which we experienced consolation and allowing them to determine the shape and direction of our lives as we move into the future. In this process, perhaps the most important gift that we need is trust. What we are effectively doing is handing over control of our lives to God, to a greater or lesser degree, saying, 'Thy will be done.' In that case, it is well to be prepared for surprises: casting off the mooring rope and moving with the Spirit may mean beaching in unexpected places.

Handling desolation

Dealing with desolation in ourselves and in others is often a more difficult matter than acting on consolation. The way forward depends to some extent upon the type of desolation in question, its probable source and how it seems to operate. The most important thing, as we have said, is as far as possible to prevent the desolation from ruling our choices and actions, for its effect is corrosive for ourselves and our relationships with others. Carrying out this instruction, however, is often far from easy. Depending on its subtlety and severity, desolation sometimes has a hold on people and affects their behaviour before they are aware of it. And even when we have an early warning of desolation and are able to act against it, the very process of enduring and withstanding it is often wearisome.

A common and very understandable reaction to desolation – as to pain of any kind – is to take evasive action or an anaesthetic: to absorb our attention and our energies in whatever at the time seems to offer solace: hard work, entertainment, eating, drinking, sleep and so forth. While this may offer temporary comfort, however, it does not in fact tackle the real issue, and in the end it is more healthy and productive of growth to face the desolation and whatever is causing it. Temporary palliatives, however, are sometimes necessary.

When we are trying to deal with desolation, knowing its cause can often help to set us free from it. The causes of desolation are many and varied. Fatigue, burn-out, stress, fear, anxiety, guilt, illness, lack of inner freedom with regard to a particular situation, 'weariness in well-doing', neglect of our relationship with God, a poor self-image, distorted images of God; all these are capable of causing desolation. Sometimes, however, it is not possible to know the cause with any certainty, in which case we can only trust that it is somehow necessary for growth in faith and discipleship (cf. Exx 322).

Ignatius Loyola and others well versed in discernment offer some tactics for dealing with desolation. The primary requirement is a belief that this experience, painful though it is, can produce good. Secondly, it is important to recognize that the workings of desolation (and temptation) are often subtle; they attack us, for example, in our most vulnerable areas (Exx 327). It is often difficult, therefore, for an individual alone to retain objectivity and clarity and to avoid being seduced by the desolation. In this case a helpful tactic is to tell a friend or a competent spiritual director about the affliction (Exx 326). The role of such a companion is twofold: to offer necessary support and encouragement to the one who is suffering, for desolation is often a lonely experience; and to help the sufferer to see more clearly and to guard against the destructive subtleties of the experience (Exx 7).

Thirdly, certain reflections can also help to counteract desolation: as, for example, recognizing the fact that the experience, however long it lasts, is temporary: experiences both of consolation and of desolation have come and gone before, and in God's good time consolation will return (Exx 321). Fourthly, it is also sound practice at these times to be sure not to make any decision or change any previous resolution of any importance (Exx 318), but to try to 'persevere in patience' (Exx 321). The reasons for this are clear from what has already been set out in this chapter: the effects of desolation are damaging, if we allow it to rule our choices, and we are not always aware of the extent to which desolation is in fact influencing us. In fact, instead of changing former decisions in accordance with the 'direction of flow' of the mood of desolation, it can be helpful to intensify our activity against it by insisting more on prayer, contemplation, reflection and penance (Exx 319). Many people find, for example, that in the right circumstances fasting is an effective antidote to serious desolation.

Finally, there are forms of desolation which are capable of luring us into a downward spiral of self-deception, false rationalization, self-absorbed feelings of guilt or remorse, or into debates within ourselves which go round and round in circles and lead nowhere. In this case two approaches are important: the first is to try to step back from the experience in order to be aware of how desolation is in fact operating (Exx 325–327); the second is to cling to God in faith and trust and not allow ourselves to be drawn into the tangled web of anxiety, argument and counter-argument (Exx 324). In fact whatever shape desolation takes, sound advice for dealing with it is to confront it boldly, and to focus not on the subtleties or power of the desolation itself but with confidence on the love and power of God (Exx 325), like Peter invited by Jesus to walk on the water (Matt. 14:22–33).

It should be noted, however, that these ways of dealing with desolation may not necessarily release us from it. That is not their main purpose; sometimes desolation is immovable and apparently has to be endured for as long as God wishes. Dealing with it in this way, however, does serve to draw its sting and lessen or prevent its destructive effects.

Experiences of desolation (and consolation for that matter) tend to fall into patterns which repeat themselves in the life of particular individuals. Reflecting on past experiences of consolation and desolation, we can sometimes discover a sequence of events and responses to them that tends to recur. Certain kinds of situation cause desolation in recognizable patterns. For some it may be exhaustion that repeatedly gives rise to desolation; for others a lack of balance between work, leisure and prayer; for others again certain relationships, the contemplation of suffering, an overwhelming sense of guilt or failure, fear, certain inner needs or compulsions, harsh or demanding images of God, and so on, all have the power to draw them into desolation. The suggestions for dealing with desolation that I have just described also help us to be on the alert for future attacks. They can help us to spot the symptoms of a recurring pattern of desolation at an early stage and thus free us from the worst effects of the experience.

CONCLUSION

The focus of this chapter has been the affective dimension of our lives. We have examined in three stages a process of noting, interpreting and acting on our experiences of consolation and desolation. This process is integral to discernment both in the current of everyday life and in regard to major choices that on particular occasions we may have to make. When described in slow motion in this way, it may seem a forbiddingly complex process. Experience shows, however, that in practice, with a little patience, it is not so, and in fact in a short time it can become almost a habit. Trying to describe in words every movement of a dance would be a relatively complex operation; for those who learn and practise them, however, the movements become almost 'second nature'.

There is one aspect of our affective lives that has a particular importance in discernment, and the next chapter will be devoted to explaining what that is and why it is important.

1   'Use your head and trust your feelings' is the title of a very valuable essay on discernment by Michael J. O'Sullivan in *Studies in the Spirituality of Jesuits*, vol. 22, no. 4 (September 1990).
2   Both of these terms offer some difficulty in contemporary usage, 'desolation' more so than 'consolation'. The problem is the breadth of the range of experiences that the terms include.

'Consolation' has long been common in spiritual writing in English to denote a wide spectrum of graced experiences ranging from a mild feeling of well-being to profound, mystical union with God. In ordinary English usage 'desolation' is usually a strong word, with connotations of barrenness, devastation and destruction, often the results of violence. It is used in discernment and spiritual direction in the Ignatian tradition to cover a very wide range of experiences, ranging from mild unease to a sense of inhabiting a barren wilderness which faith and meaning have abandoned.

3 'Spiritual' is acceptable so long as it does not carry the dualistic sense of a separate 'higher' layer or compartment of the personality, a 'ghost in the machine'. The traditional adjective 'divine' might offer an alternative to 'spiritual' were it not that 'divine desolation' suggests Marlene Dietrich in tragic mode. The more archaic and Anglo-Saxon 'godly' captures the sense that these experiences both have God as their object and are God's gift.

4 *The Spiritual Exercises* is a handbook written by Ignatius Loyola and largely devoted to setting out a programme for a retreat of thirty days. It is intended as a guide for those who are engaged in leading others through that programme and not as a self-help retreat. There are many modern translations. In references to *The Spiritual Exercises* in the rest of this book I will use the abbreviation Exx.

5

Desires

We saw in the last chapter that reflecting on our feelings, with a view to choosing the greater good, is a central feature of Christian discernment in the form in which it is bequeathed to us in the Ignatian tradition. Discernment, as we have seen, includes the ability to identify the two kinds of affective experiences that we have called 'consolation' and 'desolation', and to act upon them appropriately. In this context of discernment, however, desires have a special importance and this chapter will be devoted to explaining why this is so.

DESIRES

We might begin by noting some of the general characteristics of the desires and longings that are part of ordinary human life. Desires are aroused in us in the course of our continuing interaction with the world around us. If we were to attempt a description of desires, we might say that they are various kinds of affective movements towards (or in aversion from) objects that are known; known, that is, at least to a minimal degree. Obviously the word 'object' here does not necessarily imply something that is less than personal. We clearly can and do desire non-personal objects: children want ice cream; misers crave money; collectors have a passion for objects which to them are valuable. We also desire more abstract qualities and ideals: love, perfection, fulfilment, wisdom, justice, and so on. But to say that God or certain persons are an 'object' of desire does not necessarily demean them or make them in any way less than personal, though it can do so. A desire is an affective response which one or more of these 'objects' arouses in us and our desires move us either towards enjoyment or possession of the objects or people which evoke them or in revulsion away from them.

We often associate certain desires with particular facets of our make-up. We distinguish, for example, physical, emotional, intellectual or spiritual passions and desires according to their association with one or other aspect our human existence. In this context, however, it is important to emphasize the fact that first and foremost a human person is a unity. No doubt it is a complex, multi-dimensional unity but it is none the less a single whole. Within that unity, the different facets and dimensions of our humanity exist and act, not in isolation from each other, but in continuous interdependence. Events and changes, for example, in the social, cultural or environmental factors in our experience of the world around us have an effect upon our most personal, inner desires and longings. And what we describe as 'physical' or 'emotional' desires and passions also have intellectual and spiritual dimensions, and vice-versa. Just as the way in which we treat our bodies affects the longings of the spirit, so also the desires of the spirit find expression in our feelings and bodies.

The relevance of this to discernment lies in the fact that so-called 'spiritual' desires do not exist in a 'spiritual' compartment of life which is in some way separated from the rest. The whole of life is spiritual because, whether we recognize it or not, God is present in all of it. If a continuing relationship and dialogue with God provides the framework within which we actually live day by day, then all the desires that we experience are touched by spirit and all are matter for discernment; none is in itself irrelevant. In fact, discernment is possible because all the different dimensions of life interact and are interdependent and because God is present in all of them.

Reflection on our experience reveals that, along with other kinds of feeling, passions and desires vary greatly in intensity and strengths. They range from faint velleities to powerful passions which can take hold of us, drive us in a particular direction and govern all our thoughts, words and actions. Moreover, desires last for varying lengths of time: some are very fleeting, no more than passing fancies which have gone almost as soon as they appear, while others stay with us far longer or reappear repeatedly over the course of days, months, years.

No doubt one of the commonest human experiences is that of being pulled in different directions by our desires and passions. It is characteristic of the 'moving toyshop of the heart' that, even in a short time, we can be powerfully drawn towards people, objects or ideals that are not only widely diverse but even incompatible with each other, and moved by passions that thrust us swiftly and sometimes violently in opposite directions. Married people experience desires both for their husbands or wives and for other men or women; the same individual can feel an attraction to both poverty and wealth, family life and celibacy, self-indulgence and a life in which self is forgotten in the service of God and others. Moreover, contradictory, incompatible desires and moods not only follow each other, often in quick succession, but can also apparently be present in us at the same time. Discernment is a way of sifting through our desires and passions, so that our lives may be shaped by the best of them.

'GREAT DESIRES'

If we reflect from a Christian standpoint on the desires that have the potential to fuel and shape our choices and therefore our lives, we discover that in fact they differ widely in quality. At one end of the range, for example, are those desires for instant self-gratification in matters which are often petty and narrow. At the other end are what Ignatius Loyola used to call 'great desires': for example, the desire to be with Christ and to play one's part along with others in the struggle to establish the reign of God throughout the world, whatever the cost to oneself. In between these two poles lie a host of varied and often mutually contradictory desires.

The reflection which is part of discernment helps us first

of all to be aware of and to accept the full range of desires that we experience. That is not always easy, since there may be some desires which we do not like or are ashamed to acknowledge. Secondly it leads us to see how, in a Christian perspective, our desires vary greatly in quality. This in turn is a help towards making choices which allow our lives to be shaped by our 'great desires' rather than by those at the other end of the spectrum. The ineffectual dreamer, the man (it is usually a man) who has great visions and desires but is never able to translate them into reality, is a figure of either ridicule or pathos. So the central question for discernment is this: taking account of the circumstances in which God has placed us, how do we enable the best desires that we have to be translated into choices, actions, lifestyle?

DESIRES AND IDENTITY

The principal reason why discernment of desires is important is the intimate connection that exists between desires and personal identity. If I want to know who another person really is, knowing her history is a great help; but I also further need to understand those desires which find expression in her words and actions. The answer to the question of what, ultimately, this man or woman wants in life is one of the best clues we have to a person's true self, the mystery at the centre of each person. And that is true whether the person in question is another or oneself.

Personal discernment, as we have seen repeatedly in this book, involves becoming aware of and reflecting on our own desires within the framework of prayer and a living relationship with God. Being brought face to face with God in meditation, prayer, worship or elsewhere arouses desires in us, sometimes in opposition to God, at other times perhaps a desire to share all our gifts with other people in love for God's sake. A person's best desires are sometimes well hidden below a confusing mass of more superficial but often more clamorous or insistent wants, needs and longings. When this is so, it takes time, patience, guidance and the right kind of circumstances for those authentic desires to be discovered. But gradually the processes of reflection that I have already described help us to note the variety and the sometimes conflicting nature of our desires; to distinguish them, from a Christian standpoint, according to their quality; and they help us to ensure that as far as possible our choices and actions express the best desires that we have, and not the worst.

Given the intimate connection between desires and identity, discernment has two very important consequences. Firstly, if our desires reveal who we are – and that includes both the light and the shadow sides of us – then one of the values of the reflection involved in discernment is that it helps us to see our true self. It gets below the masks that we wear for the benefit of ourselves and others, it puts us in touch with who we really are. Secondly, it helps us to become what God desires us to be. Our best desires, which are not narrowly concerned with ourselves but with the reign of God, reflect God's own desires for the world and for each individual in it. They translate into the terms of our own circumstances God's hopes and longings for us. Our 'great desires', therefore, put us in tune with God's desires and express what God wants us to become. Discernment has to do with trying to ensure that our best desires do not remain unfulfilled but are transformed into choices, in such a way that what we say and do becomes a living expression of our best desires. Since our 'great desires' are the same as God's desires, then, when we translate them into choices and action, we enter into a process of becoming what God desires us to be. Discernment of our desires, therefore, not only reveals to us who we really are, but also enables us to see and to become what God ultimately wants us to be.

DISCERNMENT OF DESIRES

Our desires are part of life, and life is a gift from God. God made each of us as creatures with desires and longings which provide the energy and impetus for making choices and undertaking courses of action. Some of our desires are in tune with God's desires for us, while others are not. Any process of discernment rests on the belief that God wants us, not to be helplessly pushed and dragged hither and yon by conflicting desires, but to be able, at least to some degree, to choose which of our many desires we will allow and which we will not allow to give shape and direction to our lives as a whole.

In the previous chapter I described a process of sifting feelings, desires and other elements of our affective life. The desires which are significant for following the leading of the Spirit in the path of the gospel are those which, whether directly or indirectly, have to do with God, with God's dealings with the world, or with us personally. Clearly some circumstances are more likely than others to arouse these desires. Prayer, meditation, worship, are settings which readily stir our deepest longings. But in fact any event or set of circumstances also has the potential to do so, since God is present in all. It is good to remind ourselves, however, that this sifting of desires is not a process of introspection. It is not a matter of searching inside ourselves in order to uncover possible motivations for our actions, whether past or present. Attention is focused on the desires and longings which we find in ourselves, the moods they create in us and the direction in which they move us, rather than on the possible roots or motives of our actions. Desires which create consolation are in tune with God's desires for us, while those which put us into desolation are not. Distinguishing desires in this way in turn enables us to act appropriately on them, according to whether we experience them as consolation or desolation.

The purpose of reflecting on and sifting our desires in discernment, therefore, is to enable us to distinguish the authentic from the bogus, the deeper from the more superficial, our best desires from those which are less good, the desires of the true self from those of the false, those which are in tune with God's desires from those which are not. This reflection also aims at recognizing the difference between choices made in freedom on the one hand and, on the other hand, those based on perhaps unconscious needs or compulsions, which tend to control us and restrict the scope of effective freedom.

81

This sifting of our desires and longings helps us to grow towards a condition in which those desires which are authentic expressions of our true selves shape and fuel our choices and actions.

An example will help to illustrate this process. Suppose I feel that I am at a turning point in my life and I am trying to decide which direction my next steps should take. Perhaps I experience a renewed call to follow the Spirit in the path of the gospel. Among the relevant factors on which I reflect are: the options available to me and the advantages and disadvantages of each; the circumstances, needs, thoughts and feelings of people close to me, such as my immediate family or my community; my own endowments and capabilities; the needs that others have of the service I can offer; the life, death and resurrection of Jesus, and so on. But giving attention to the deepest desires that contemplation both of the gospels and of this situation evokes in me is also an especially important part of this discernment process. It may be that I am a parent and what I want most of all is to contribute to the reign of God through my family life. On the other hand, if I am a single person with considerable freedom and few dependants, I may find in myself at this moment of change a profound longing to join with others in standing alongside those who are poor. These desires, which come to the surface when I am brought face to face with God and the reality of life, are important signs of where a good choice lies in these circumstances. They are an indication both of who I really am and of what I am called by God to be.

DESIRES AND NEEDS

For the purpose of understanding discernment, it is also good to recall that alongside desires we also have needs, and that between desires and needs there are both likenesses and differences. So far we have been discussing mainly conscious desires, but desires and needs may be both conscious and unconscious. Both conscious and unconscious desires and needs can supply the necessary drive and energy to move us to choose and to act. If I want or need money or love, and I am aware that I want or need them, those are conscious desires and needs. On the other hand, my behaviour can also be influenced by forces within me of which I am not aware but which also move me towards having money or love (or anything else for that matter). It is to these that the term unconscious applies.

It is not unusual for us to experience a conflict between conscious and unconscious desires and needs. A businessman, for example, might come to a point at which he discovers that his life is dominated by a need to succeed and to be seen to succeed in the business world, a need of which he was previously unaware. At the same time, if he looks at his conscious desires, he may find that what he really wants is a life of domestic family peace in the heart of the country, far away from the rat-race. Perhaps that unconscious need to succeed in the eyes of others is what drives him to stay in business, though he detests its competitiveness, its values and its prizes. But he is trapped by a hitherto unconscious need which drives him to behave in a way which he detests.

In discernment, both individually and in a group, time given to becoming aware of unconscious needs and desires which may be governing some aspects of our behaviour is rarely time wasted. There are several reasons for this. First of all, in certain circumstances, when we are faced with choices, if unconscious needs or desires are powerful and influential, they affect our perceptions and behaviour. Suppose, for example, much of my life is under the sway of a need, present from childhood but as yet unconscious, not to go against anyone who happens to be in a position of authority. In this case many of my perceptions and choices in different circumstances are likely to be influenced by that need, though I am not aware of the fact. A second reason for taking steps to become aware of our as yet unconscious needs or desires lies in the fact that they engender corresponding fears. Let us suppose in this case that Frances is a member of a religious congregation and, though she is unaware of it, much of her behaviour is dominated by an unconscious need to be seen by others to succeed in whatever she undertakes in the world of work. This need has its corresponding fear: that of not succeeding, or of not appearing to succeed; the fear of failure. If Frances is a member of a community or chapter that is discussing mission, this need and its accompanying fear are liable to govern the ways in which she participates in a group and to colour any perceptions that she has, or choices that she favours, as regards mission. Dominant, though unconscious, needs and fears can be enemies of fruitful discernment, because they so easily give rise to distorted perceptions and judgements and can paralyse creative choices.

The purpose of reflecting in such a way that we become aware of the unconscious needs and fears that can dominate our judgements and choices is not so that we might rid ourselves of them entirely. That is neither desirable, since they are potential sources of energy and by no means all destructive, nor possible. The Spirit can blow through unconscious needs and desires as well as through those that are conscious. The important thing is not to have no unconscious drives but to know what they are. Becoming aware of them serves to reduce their power to drive us helplessly like leaves before the wind. From the point of view of discernment, therefore, the aim of recognizing and reflecting on unconscious needs and desires, is to be able to sift them, as always in the context of a continuing dialogue with God; to distinguish those which are truly creative and liberating (sources of consolation) from those which are oppressive or destructive (sources of desolation); and to harness the energies of consolation for courses of action or ways of living which embody the greater good that we truly desire. By this means we are in a better position to cooperate with the Spirit in giving shape to our lives instead of being at the mercy of unconscious drives.

6

To love as Jesus loved

In the previous two chapters we have looked closely at the part played in Christian discernment by the affective dimension of our nature: our moods, feelings, desires, affections, longings, and so forth. But that was based on the understanding that this is not the whole picture. As well as being a creature of feeling, a human person also engages in understanding, logical argument, reflection, judgement and evaluation. We are made up of both 'heart' and 'head'. In this chapter, therefore, we are turning our attention first of all to the equally important role in discernment of this dimension of our existence and activity. By temperament, heredity and natural inclination, some people appear to be ruled by their hearts, others by their heads. The Christian tradition of discernment strives for a balanced partnership of the two.

UNDERSTANDING, JUDGING, EVALUATING

Our capacity to understand, to make judgements and to engage in reflection comes into play in discernment in three ways. The first has to do with gathering information. Discernment is about making choices, and choices are only valid when they are well-informed. For fruitful discernment, therefore, as for any process of decision-making, it is essential to have as much accurate information as is possible about all the relevant factors, so that an informed choice can be made. In practice, this exploratory exercise sometimes results in a change in the range of available options, by revealing that what at first sight appeared to be possible options are not in fact viable, or by introducing other options which had not previously been considered. But both in everyday choices and in major decisions, having adequate information about the options available and the circumstances surrounding them is very important. Discernment founders if it is based on inadequate information.

A second area, obviously, in which our capacity to understand, to reason, to contrast and weigh one thing against another and to form judgements has a part to play is the process of reflection on our affective responses to life and to God that we have discussed in the last two chapters. That process presupposes a certain capacity to step back from one's own feelings in order to interpret and weigh them.

In any responsible decision-making, from the Cabinet to the family conference round the kitchen table, when people are faced with a choice between a number of different options, it is sensible to state and discuss all the reasons that can be thought of both for and against each of them. This, then, is the third way in which our minds are engaged in a process of discernment. It is a matter, first of all, of listing all the reasons and arguments both for and against each of the possible options. In practical terms, the following has been found to be a helpful method: (1) to take one of the possible options; (2) to consider carefully all the reasons and arguments in favour of this option; (3) to consider all the reasons and arguments against this option. (4) To repeat this process with each of the options until one reaches a choice based on these considerations. The fact that one option has numerically more reasons in its favour does not necessarily imply, of course, that this option is the one to choose. The important question is the weight or value of the reasons or arguments on each side in relation to each other. The process of sifting can be relatively slow, as now one, now another consideration seems more important. The aim eventually, however, is to arrive at a sense of which option has the greater weight of reasons and arguments in its favour.

Normally this process of weighing the reasons and arguments about a choice works in conjunction with the process of sifting experiences of consolation and desolation. It does happen sometimes, however, that a person deliberating a decision does not seem to experience any affective responses either of consolation or desolation. It may be that the choice has to be made purely on rational grounds, but the situation requires careful handling. If a person is praying in a way that truly brings her into contact with the word of God, one would expect her to experience consolation and/or desolation, since these are no more than our affective responses to God, when God is mediated to us in the biblical text or in some other form. There is the possibility, however, that, consciously or unconsciously, when we are faced with a decision, we will try to avoid or resist any consideration of feelings, because they may be painful, and try to keep all discussion at a rational or intellectual level, because that seems safer and offers less of a threat. In this case, meditative prayer which brings us in some way into contact with the word of God is particularly important because it creates a setting in which we can 'move from the head to the heart', and affective responses, whether of consolation or desolation, can be gently aroused.

THE NEED FOR A NORM

In this chapter we are mainly concerned with the part played in discernment by our capacity to understand, reason logically, compare and weigh different considerations and form judgements based on rational arguments. If we are engaged in weighing the relative importance of different factors such as reasons or arguments for or against certain options – if, that is to say, we want to be in a position to say that from a Christian point of view one consideration or option is more weighty than another – we need an acceptable norm by which to make this evaluation. We need to be able to state the grounds on which a judgement like this is based. To put it more concretely, suppose I am engaged in making a major decision about my future, and one of my options is to go to live and work in South Africa. When I am weighing the relative importance of reasons for and against this particular option, I need a value or norm which will enable me to decide whether, for example, offering pastoral support to certain groups of people in South Africa in these times of political and social upheaval is more or less important than teaching and writing books in London. Our discussion of discernment is therefore moving on to an examination of the criteria which we might use in order to weigh the relative importance of options, reasons and arguments which come to light in the process of reflection.

Let me state the question again in slightly different terms. Discernment allows us to choose and put into effect that option which we believe represents, in the circumstances within which we are making a choice, the greater good. (Alternatively if, as sometimes happens, circumstances unavoidably offer us only a choice between two or more evils, then the aim is to choose the lesser evil.) This means making a judgement as to which of the options available embodies the greater good. And in order to make such a judgement, we need a norm of goodness upon which it can be based. In other words, if I judge that, all things considered, in these particular circumstances option X represents a greater good (or a lesser evil) than option Y or Z, I need to be able to say why I judge this to be so; I need to be able to state the grounds on which my evaluation is based.

We have already seen that experiences of consolation and desolation offer some grounds on which to base judgements. For those who are genuinely trying to live the gospel and to be open to the Spirit, experiences of consolation indicate where the greater good lies; while experiences of desolation will tend to draw us away from the greater good. These, however, important though they are, are personal and subjective grounds for judgements. Quite apart from these, we also need more external and objective criteria by which we can make such an evaluation. We need to be able to say 'I believe X is a greater good than Y because . . .' and offer reasons, quite apart from our own personal feelings, which other people can recognize as valid.

In the section of *The Spiritual Exercises* which is devoted to the process of making a good choice, Ignatius Loyola set out what he believed to be the main foundation on which to base judgements about the goodness of different options. Throughout the different exercises that he proposes to help those who are faced with a choice, the norm that he suggests is a constant one: to choose that option which in the circumstances we believe will give 'greater praise and glory' to God:

> I should be like a balance at equilibrium, without leaning to either side, that I might be ready to follow whatever I perceive is more for the glory and praise of God our Lord and for the salvation of my soul (Exx 179). (Cf. also Exx 152; 169; 180; 189.)

The logic of this, in the mind of Ignatius, is straightforward. To put it in his own terms, he believed that the purpose for which each of us was created is to 'give praise, reverence and service to God' in all that we are and do (Exx 23). In his guidelines for making a decision, Ignatius assumes that a person is faced with a choice between two or more options, either of which, if put into effect, would 'give praise, reverence and service to God'. A discerning choice, therefore, would be to choose that option which that person believes would give *greater* 'praise and glory' to God.

In the course of making the Spiritual Exercises, when those who are faced with a choice come to the point of considering this norm, they are also engaged in constant meditation on the gospel story of the life, ministry, death and resurrection of Jesus. They place themselves in imagination in different scenes from the gospels and allow the story of the life and ministry of Jesus to shed light on the options before them, in order to guide them to a right choice. It is the gospel story, therefore, that helps them to spell out in a given situation which of the available options would give 'greater praise and glory to God'.

TO LOVE AS JESUS LOVED

I would like to suggest that the principal norm on which these judgements of relative importance may be based is the love which we find embodied in the life, ministry, death and resurrection of Jesus. That is to say, if we are considering the relative weight of various reasons for or against a particular option, reason X will be seen, from a Christian standpoint, as more important than Y if it embodies more fully the love that is shown forth in the life, ministry, death and resurrection of Jesus. Similarly, that option is the greater good which, all things considered, appears most fully to represent that love in the circumstances in which we are placed. Then we are in a position to say that P is more weighty than Q because there the love which Jesus embodies shines out more completely. Alternatively, since the gospel metaphor of the reign of God sums up the meaning and purpose of Jesus' life and expresses all the many facets of the love which shaped it, the reign of God in the fullness of its gospel meaning may also be taken as a norm of judgement in discernment. In that case, P may be seen as more important than Q, or as containing a greater good than Q, because P comes closer to embodying in particular circumstances the reign of God.

Perhaps it is also important to note how we are approaching this question. It is not a matter of following the path of a 'perfectionist spirituality' and saying: 'We find in the life, death and resurrection of Jesus a general or abstract ideal of perfect love and strive in all circumstances to reach that ideal.' Our present approach is different. It entails, in a framework of prayer based on the word of God, considering all the factors in the situation which seem to be relevant to making a good choice, including experiences of consolation and desolation and the reasons for and against each of the available options; and secondly on that basis choosing that option which, taking into consideration all the possibilities and limitations of our given circumstances, most fully expresses the love manifest in the life, ministry, death and resurrection of Jesus, most fully embodies the reign of God.

Jesus' ministry was shaped by love. All the gospels portray

90

him as a man who recognized that everything comes from God as free gift. His ministry and his death express his own personal response to that love. They show him as a person whose existence was shaped, on the one hand, by his awareness of the extent and quality of God's love for the world, its people and himself as an individual, and on the other hand by that 'rule of love' which is his own response to God's love: 'You must love the Lord your God with all your heart, with all your soul, with all your mind and with all your strength . . . You must love your neighbour as yourself. There is no commandment greater than these' (Mark 12:30 and parallels).

From the gospel accounts of Jesus' ministry it is clear that he was unusually sensitive and responsive to human need and suffering in any form, which is surely the mark of one whose view of the world is shaped by God's love. Perhaps the gospel stories in which the most needy gather round him when he is still and follow him when he travels reflect the fact that in Jesus they recognized a man who not only helped them but also understood them, accepted them and was one with them in a rare and extraordinary way. He is described as being criticized for sharing a table with the neediest, the poorest and the least loved (Mark 2:15, etc.), and for allowing his feet to be washed by 'a woman of the town' (Luke 7:36–50). His love for them and for all seems to have led him to share with them everything that he had received from God. He shared his gifts, however, not as a philanthropist who from a sheltered position of wealth doles out benefactions to the less fortunate, but as a man who recognized that his true place was within the circle of fragile, needy humankind and who, from that position, placed all that he was and all that he had at the service of his sisters and brothers, and especially of those among them whose needs were greatest (Mark 10:41–45). The stories of Jesus sharing his food with crowds (Mark 6:30–44; 8:1–10 and parallels), and his action, described in the Fourth Gospel, of washing his disciples' feet, witness to the presence and power of this love in Jesus' life.

The cross of Jesus is a symbol *par excellence* of Jesus' love; it expresses both the nature and the quality of that love.

91

When his love was challenged by his enemies and the hunt began, he could have withdrawn; possibly at any time up to his death he could have recanted and saved himself. But in fact he continued to love whatever the cost might be, to assert the value of the love that had shaped all his ministry, and for it he paid the price in full.

Theologians state that Jesus helps humankind to understand itself. That is to say, in the life, death and resurrection of Jesus we have a picture of what God desires humanity, collectively and individually, to be; in Jesus we have a pattern of what it means to be truly human. Since the kind of love that I have briefly described here was what gave shape and direction to Jesus' life, it follows that to love as Jesus loved is the way to fulfilling God's desires for us, the way to becoming what God desires us to be. In discernment, as we have seen, there are two forms of reflection, two sets of factors, which together are used to guide choices. Reflection on experiences of consolation and desolation offers a personal, subjective guide for giving shape and direction to our choices. On the other hand, the love which animated and guided the life of Jesus right up to the moment of his death provides us with a more objective norm, which helps us to assess the relative weight of various reasons for or against the options available to us and thus gradually to arrive at a sense of the importance of those options themselves in relation to each other. Through these two forms of reflection, working in union with each other, it is possible to 'have the mind (and the heart) of Christ' (Phil. 2:5–11), in the sense of allowing that love which shaped Jesus' life to shape ours also. This is to take part in the dance of the Spirit and to set ourselves on the path towards becoming, both collectively and individually, the people God desires and invites us to be.

THE FOOLISHNESS OF GOD AS THE NORM OF DISCERNMENT

The love which shaped the life of Jesus led him to the cross, and the cross is the symbol *par excellence* of that love. Our discussion in this chapter has thus led us to a point which we have already reached more than once before in this book, but by different paths. The death of Jesus is the sign of the wisdom and the love of God which is a scandal and a folly to ordinary, conventional human ways of thinking and acting. The cross and the love which it expresses support the claim that God's ways are not our ways, nor God's thoughts our thoughts. In discernment, as we have seen, when consolation is genuine it draws us to follow the pattern of Jesus' love which is the way of the cross. When this same love is also accepted as the less purely subjective norm which also guides our choices, then our lives are shaped by that same mysterious wisdom of God. Christian discernment, therefore, does not limit itself to what prudence or common sense dictates. That is not to say, obviously, that prudence and common sense are excluded; as we have seen, they have a part to play in discernment, and in fact the way of prudence is sometimes also the way of genuine Christian love. The ultimate guide for our choices is not primarily prudence, a particular ideology or conventional wisdom, but our own appreciation of what it means in practice here and now to love as Jesus loved. That is the music which shapes the dance.

LOVE AND JUSTICE

Love has to do with the ways in which people treat others whose lives they touch directly. Living as a Christian means trying to ensure that all our interpersonal dealings are governed by the kind of love that Jesus preached and practised. Moreover, loving as Jesus loved also includes justice, because it means treating other people, whoever they may be, with the respect and dignity which is due to them as daughters and sons of the Father and brothers and sisters of Jesus.

There are those who would say that Christian love is, and should be, concerned only with the inter-personal aspect of life. One of the recent developments in our understanding of what it means to be a Christian, however, is a widespread and growing awareness that this love also has an institutional and structural dimension and that this is, moreover, an integral part of genuine Christian love and not an added optional extra. The lives of all of us are sustained by social and cultural systems, structures and institutions. These factors create for those who depend upon them conditions of either justice, peace, freedom and love, or else injustice, servitude, exploitation and oppression. Loving as Jesus loved, therefore, also means that each of us, in our own circumstances and with the gifts God has given to us, is called to make a contribution to creating and maintaining a world in which all people, whoever they are, enjoy a quality of life which is in keeping with their dignity as sons and daughters of the Father and sisters and brothers of Jesus.

In our understanding of Christian love, we are in a time of transition. In our practice of discernment today, when we look to love as the norm by which to guide our choices, it would surely be wrong to limit our perceptions of what that love is to the area of interpersonal relationships. It is increasingly recognized that the call to be a Christian today also includes an appeal to each of us, within the limitations of our own circumstances and our own gifts, to help to create a world in which social and cultural structures and institutions also embody and foster the love and justice which Jesus preached and practised. This surely needs to be a major consideration in all our judgements about the relative importance of the options which face us in discernment, both in day-to-day choices and in major decisions. To love in the world of today as Jesus loved means giving due weight to those options which engage us, in so far as is possible for each one, in creating a society and culture which will enable all, whoever they are, to enjoy the justice and freedom of sons and daughters of the Father.

PRACTICAL WAYS OF MAKING A CHOICE

At various stages of this explanation of discernment I have emphasized the fundamental unity of the human individual and the fact that the two dimensions of our lives that we have examined, the affective and the rational, are not in practice separable from each other but interact and work together. In these last three chapters, however, we have focused our attention on the affective and rational dimensions of all our activity somewhat in isolation from each other, largely for reasons of clarity and emphasis. I wish to conclude this chapter with a description of the practice of discernment in which the affective and rational aspects of us work together. We are putting Humpty Dumpty together again. Three examples will serve as illustrations.

(1) Bridget and Matthew are married with two children, one nine, the other eleven. Matthew is a plumber. Before they had children, Bridget worked as a catering manager in a school, but when their first child was born, she gave up that work and since then has been a full-time housewife and mother. Now that the children are older and at school all day, Bridget has felt a desire to start going out to work again, or at least to do something other than being a full-time housewife. Both she and Matthew feel that it is an important decision and have given the question prayerful consideration together. Eventually Matthew tells Bridget that he will gladly accept whatever she decides to do. Bridget has a period of quiet, meditative prayer almost every day, usually with a focus on a passage in the New Testament, and at the beginning of each of these sessions she, as it were, brings the question to God and places it in God's hands and leaves it there. From time to time she also notes and reflects on the feelings that she experiences over a period of time with regard to each of the possible options open to her; she gives particular attention to the feelings which arise in her prayer. She finds that she runs through a wide variety of feelings: from enthusiasm, encouragement, gratitude, peace, to fear, guilt, anxiety, discouragement, and so on. On one or two evenings, after the children have gone to bed, she sits down with a pen and paper and writes down all the reasons that she can think of both in favour of and against the available options. She finds that she wants to make that choice which seems to her to express the love that she finds in the life and death of Jesus. Gradually it is the cumulative effect of her experiences of

consolation together with the relative weight of reasons and arguments that lead her to choose a particular option. Even once the decision has been made, she still brings it in the same way into her regular prayer; when she does that she feels that the choice she has made is in harmony with herself, her family and her best desires for all of them. Gradually her fears, guilt and anxiety about the decision diminish.

(2) Maggie and Ken live on a run-down housing estate on the outskirts of a large city. The housing complex was put up in the 'fifties when the city-centre slums were being cleared. It is a multi-racial area with a high level of unemployment. Ken and Maggie have been married six years and have two small children. Ken was made redundant four and a half years ago and has not been able to get a job since then. Being a housewife and mother takes up most of Maggie's time. She is also a regular churchgoer and enjoys attending a small weekly prayer group for young mothers at the local convent. There she has learned more about the Bible than she ever learned at school, and has been taught how to pray using stories from the gospels, which she enjoys doing at home whenever she can find a quiet corner. Being unemployed for several years has had a bad effect on Ken: he always liked a drink, but in the last year he has turned into a heavy drinker. He spends an increasing amount of time away from the house, and on two occasions he raised his hand to strike Maggie. She and Ken have tried to talk to each other calmly about the whole situation but that does not seem to do much lasting good. After a series of fierce arguments Maggie begins to consider seriously whether she and the children should live apart from Ken. She brings this into her prayer and is surprised at the strength of the feelings that come to the surface: anger because she feels that she has never really been able to find herself as an individual woman in her own right; anger about the social conditions which keep her and her family in poverty; anger against the church which seems to accept those conditions so readily; sadness for her husband who is trapped in so many ways; guilt and a crippling sense of failure when she thinks about leaving Ken and about the marriage vows

they made; elation at the thought of being free from Ken's drinking and then guilt because she feels elated; fear about a future either with Ken or without him. All these and many other feelings crowd in on her. She talks about her feelings with the prayer group leader, who in turn shows Maggie how, when she is feeling calm, she can also think clearly about the reasons why she should or should not leave Ken. Gradually, through praying with the gospels and struggling for a long time with her feelings and thoughts, Maggie makes her decision. Having decided what she would do, Maggie feels generally peaceful in herself, but is still liable to times of fear, anger, guilt and so on.

(3) Frank is a foreman in an engineering company. Two or three times a week he finds a quiet fifteen minutes for a prayerful review of his everyday life. He also reads passages from the gospels or the psalms fairly regularly. In his review, with a spirit of gratitude for the gift of his life and all that it contains, he recalls the events of the previous two or three days and his experiences of consolation and desolation in response to those events. He looks at the everyday choices he makes; he tries to see where the Spirit of God has been leading him and how he has acted in response; he tries to act upon his experiences of consolation and not to allow his choices to be shaped by desolation; he also looks at the harmonies and disharmonies between his own life and that of Jesus in the gospels, and finds himself asking: what would Jesus do in these circumstances? He has been praying in this way regularly for about three years now, and notices how much his life has slowly but definitely changed in that time.

These three examples illustrate the main practical features of a process of making choices through discernment within a context of prayer. I would like to make a few further comments on them. First, the immediate framework for the decision is regular prayer which is nourished in some way by the Bible, and especially the New Testament. In this way the word of God and especially the love manifest in the life, death and resurrection of Jesus provide a perspective which helps to guide choices. Secondly, in each case reflection on experiences of consolation and desolation, and reflection on the reasons for or against various options, interact and work together, so that the choice ultimately arises out of their cumulative effect. In example (3), however, the small choices of every day obviously do not need the same degree of deliberate consideration as is necessary for the major choices which face Bridget and Maggie, since Frank is very familiar with the day-to-day circumstances of his own life. Thirdly, it is worth noting that this process of discernment is not guaranteed to give absolute certainty. The cumulative effect offers strong probability and sometimes a degree of inner certainty which will be confirmed and strengthened by subsequent experience. But the fact that a choice is made through a process of discernment by no means rules out the possibility that doubts, fears or anxieties will recur. All our choices and their consequences have to be lived out in faith and trust.

7

Group discernment

So far in this book we have concentrated mainly on individual discernment: individual people making choices and endeavouring to be faithful to the Spirit of God both in the course of daily life and when faced with particularly important decisions. Though we have recognized throughout the previous chapters that each Christian is constituted by a complex network of social, cultural and ecclesial relationships and that he or she makes choices within a particular social, cultural and ecclesial milieu, none the less our primary focus has been the individual person and her or his attempts to live by the Spirit of God in the path of the gospel. In this chapter, however, we turn our attention to forms or practices of group discernment. By that I mean processes in which the members of a group or community are invited to participate fully in making decisions which affect the lives either of particular individuals or of the whole group.

A BROADER CONTEXT

Obviously many varied forms of group decision-making have been developed over a long period of time in all cultures. Some of these appear to be linked with religious aspects of a culture, others are more or less exclusively 'secular'. In our contemporary Western society we have a wide range of such decision-making practices, by which responsibility for choices is shared among a group of people all of whom have a part to play in the process: committees, boards, commissions, networks, cabinets, parliaments, elections, referenda, to name but a few.

Similarly in the Christian community there is no shortage of processes of decision-making in which members of a group participate and share responsibility for choices. The Christian churches themselves have long recognized the need for various levels and forms of assemblies, conferences, synods and councils, both local and international, for the purposes of government and decision-making. Since the Reformation, many Protestant communities, especially those in the Presbyterian, Congregationalist and Methodist traditions, have evolved their own forms and processes of decision-making in which the members of the local community have an important part to play. In the monastic orders the chapter has been an integral part of the structure of everyday life at least since the time of St Benedict. Other communities of religious with fewer monastic structures and practices have adopted chapter government or had it imposed on them by ecclesiastical authority, with appropriate degrees and styles of adaptation. And the Religious Society of Friends (Quakers) is notable for having evolved its own very distinct method of communal decision-making.[1]

The form of communal decision-making that we shall examine in this chapter, therefore, is one among many different processes in which members of a Christian group or community share responsibility for choices which affect both their own lives and the lives of a wider circle of people. At the same time, it has its own particular features which mark it out as different from many other forms of Christian decision-making. When I call it a process of communal discernment I am using the words in a very precise sense. The term 'communal discernment' is sometimes used more loosely to describe a variety of forms of Christian decision-making in which a group of people participates and in which some more or less explicit reference is made to the presence or guidance of the Holy Spirit. The fact that the participants firmly believe in the presence of the Spirit, and sing the *Veni Creator* or spend a few moments in silent prayer at the beginning of the proceedings does not automatically make the process one of 'discernment' in the precise sense in which we have been using it in this book.

The specific features of the form of communal discernment that I shall sketch in this chapter will of course become clear as we proceed. At this point, however, it may be appropriate to mention what distinguishes it fundamentally from other forms of Christian decision-making. That is, it is a process which transfers to the setting of a group the method of individual discernment that we have been discussing in detail in this book. That is to say, the explicit aim of the process, and therefore the group's primary focus of attention, is to 'find the will of God'; to discover and follow where the Spirit of God is leading in the group.

In the present climate in the church, there are signs of a growing need to find and develop communal forms of discernment. This need is not, of course, a new one. Engaged and married couples, or pairs and groups of friends, often informally practise 'group discernment' when they share with each other their thoughts and deepest feelings about a question which is important to them. And to watch a 'family conference' in action can sometimes be an education in communal discernment! Nevertheless, there are occasions when a need is felt for a systematic process of group discernment which a group or community can use and adapt for its own circumstances. In some parish groups, for example, the responsibility for decisions which affect the parish no longer lies exclusively in the hands of the parish priest. In many prayer and faith-sharing groups the members collectively take responsibility for the shape and direction of the life of the whole group. Moreover, one of the contemporary 'signs of the times' is the emergence of new forms of Christian communities, involving lay people, clergy and religious, whose members have or would like to have communal discernment as an inbuilt structural feature of their collective life. And in recent years many religious congregations have looked for and written into their revised constitutions new processes and structures of 'shared responsibility' which are more participatory than the older monarchical structures based on authority exercised from above. There is no doubt that in these and other situations a need is felt for communal discernment.

THE IGNATIAN TRADITION OF COMMUNAL DISCERNMENT

Extant records from the life of Ignatius contain a document, 'The Deliberations of the First Fathers', which mentions a process of communal discernment of God's will used by Ignatius and his companions in Rome in 1538/9. This will be the main basis for our discussion of group discernment in this chapter. The document, however, provides only a sketch and not a step-by-step description of the process used by Ignatius' group. If it is to be useful as a model for us, therefore, it has to be filled out with details drawn from what we know of Ignatian discernment from other sources such as *The Spiritual Exercises* and Ignatius' 'Autobiography'.[2]

The historical context: Rome 1538–40

It is important to have some understanding of the historical context of the process of discernment which this document describes. The group had been formed in the course of the previous few years while Ignatius was a student at the University of Paris. Ignatius seems to have been the centre of the group and its natural leader; he was older than the others, and the group formed around him and under his personal influence. The members of the group differed from one another greatly in several respects: France and Spain were then hostile towards each other and the group brought together men from both countries; the temperaments of such men as Francis Xavier and Pierre Favre, for example, two of the group, were as different as their social origins: Pierre came from a poor family in the mountains of Savoy, while Francis prided himself on the nobility of his Basque pedigree. The members of the group were drawn together not simply by ties of natural friendship but also by the discovery of shared religious desires, ideals and purposes, largely through the

102

influence of Ignatius. All had made the Spiritual Exercises under Ignatius' guidance.

By the end of their studies in Paris they were a group of committed men intent on devoting themselves with enthusiasm to the service of God. At that time they all made vows of poverty and chastity and left Paris in pairs, committed to one of two courses of action. Their first desire was to go to preach the gospel in Jerusalem; but if that were not possible, they agreed that they would go to Rome and offer themselves to the Pope to be sent wherever he wished them to go. Since, as it happened, it was not possible for them to go to Jerusalem, they made their way, on foot, to Rome.

Once gathered in Rome, Ignatius and his companions found themselves faced with a choice. Should they, on the one hand, offer their services to the Pope simply as a band of individuals, with the likelihood that they would be dispersed to all the 'round earth's imagined corners' and the group would be broken up? Or should they bind themselves together by some more permanent ties and so preserve the unity that they already had? In concrete terms, should they establish themselves as a religious order? As there were tensions in the group, a decision was not easy. In the end they agreed upon a method of communal discernment which they trusted would enable them to find what God desired for them as a group and thus to shape their future.

The process

Using this document and what we know from other sources of Ignatius' practice of discernment, we may work out the principal steps of the method used on this occasion.[3] (1) There was a common basis for discernment upon which all were agreed, namely to look for where the Spirit was leading the group; to search for the will of God. (2) It was known that individual members of the group had differences of opinion as to how to achieve this end. (3) Each member of the group gave himself up to prolonged and assiduous prayer and meditation in order to receive enlightenment from God. In one phase of the process, when it was proving difficult to arrive at a common decision about obedience, the members of the group did not speak to each other outside their meetings but sought personal enlightenment from the Holy Spirit. (4) They also used all natural means of enlightenment, such as being as fully informed as possible about the situation about which they were making their choices. (5) Taking care to be as objective as possible, each member of the group, after his own individual prayer and discernment, decided in freedom his own conclusion about the option under consideration. (6) The members of the group then came together to share with each other the outcome of their personal discernment in a process of common discernment. During this stage of the process each one stated with simplicity and candour the reasons which he saw against and then the reasons which he saw in favour of the option under consideration. By means of this process Ignatius and his companions arrived at their decision.

Reflections on the process

(1) The practice of group decision-making which derives from Ignatius Loyola has two distinguishing features which we would do well to keep in mind. In the first place, it is a process of *discernment* properly so-called. The primary aim of communal discernment is not to reach the most sensible or prudent decision, or the one which is most acceptable to a majority, or the option which has received the most persuasive backing in debate and discussion. Ignatian discernment is not simply an exercise in democracy or majority rule. Though the process may be 'democratic' in the sense that each partici-pant has an equal voice and vote, and though decisions reached by this process may in fact turn out to be sensible, prudent and popular with the majority, the primary and explicit aim of the process is to enable the group to be aware of, to invoke and to respond faithfully to the presence and movement of the Spirit of God, and thus to 'find God's will' for the group. Each element of the process is intended to work towards this end.

(2) Ignatius' group, therefore, seem to have transferred the principles and method of individual discernment, as outlined for example in *The Spiritual Exercises*, to the setting of a group, at the same time making such adaptations as were thought necessary. All the important elements of individual discernment find a place here: serious and often prolonged prayer; as thorough a knowledge of the situation as is possible in the circumstances; freedom as regards the possible outcome of the discernment; noting and sifting the reasons both for and against the options and the experiences of consolation and desolation of those who are making the decision; an experience of confirmation or of its opposite, further confusion and inner conflict.

(3) As in individual discernment, so also here in this group process, the past points to the future. In individual discernment, a person's history and the identity which is established through that history are important pointers to the shape of his or her future, and a guide to the choices to be made. Choices are made on the basis of one's history appropriated in faith. In communal discernment the shared history of the group has a similar importance. In our example of Ignatius and his companions, the writer of the 'Deliberations of the First Fathers' document sees the fact that the group had come together and grown in friendship as a sign of the hand of God and as a reason why they should form bonds of permanent union among themselves.

(4) It is very important that the aim and ground rules of this process of communal discernment are known and accepted beforehand by all those taking part. This reduces the scope for manipulation by individuals or factions in the group or for moving the goalposts. Experience suggests that it is particularly important that all should also agree beforehand the kind of consensus that will constitute an acceptable decision. This might involve stipulating, for example: whether and under what circumstances there is to be voting; whether unanimity is necessary; and what constitutes a sufficient majority.

(5) Contemporary experience also shows that the presence of a facilitator, who is not a member of the group and therefore

not one of the decision-makers, can be extremely helpful. The facilitator's responsibility is to enable the group to carry through the process according to the agreed ground rules, and, where necessary, to be a source of both encouragement and objective insight. The facilitator's role as regards the group is very similar to that of the director as regards the individual in the discernment process that takes place in the course of the Spiritual Exercises.

(6) The process used by Ignatius and his companions ensures that each person in the group has the opportunity to state clearly what he or she wishes to say both for and against all the options in question. In speaking to the options, the members of the group have no need to concentrate on such tactics as persuasive rhetoric, scoring debating points, winning votes or putting down opponents. All that is needed is to express one's thoughts and feelings on the matter in question with candour, confidence and simplicity. And since the process eliminates the kind of cut-and-thrust discussion that some might find intimidating, the process helps to ensure that members of the group are free from fears which can so easily inhibit an honest expression of one's personal thoughts and feelings.

(7) This process of group discernment calls for certain qualities in those who take part. The first is a considerable level of trust within the group, which encourages or at least allows each person to speak freely, openly and honestly. In this respect, Ignatius and his companions had the advantage of several years of friendship and a thorough knowledge of each other's strengths and weaknesses. But the trust which arose among such a varied and highly individual group of men was not won without struggle. Genuine discernment is inhibited in proportion to the lack of trust within a group. Experience also shows, however, that generous participation in group discernment itself generates and deepens trust among the members of a group. A second highly desirable quality is the ability to listen to others with openness and, as far as possible, without being swayed by bias or prejudice. Though clearly bias and prejudice can never be wholly eliminated, the inclusion in the process of a daily quota of lengthy

periods of personal prayer is designed as a help towards freeing the participants from their worst effects. Through prayer and reflection, we can become aware of our own particular biases and prejudices and take steps to ensure that they do not inhibit our ability to accept what others say or cloud our judgement.

(8) It is not wholly unusual for this process of listening humbly to others, of speaking with honesty and simplicity and of searching together for the leading of the Spirit, to bring about profound and sometimes quite dramatic changes in the viewpoints, attitudes and dispositions of the members of a group. It sometimes happens, for instance, that individuals go into the discernment process convinced that option A is the best course of action. After listening, however, to the thoughts and feelings of others and seeing the direction in which the group is gradually and often painfully moving, their views change and eventually, out of conviction, they choose the option which they had initially not favoured. For other people, taking part in communal discernment may lead to greater freedom and broader horizons, when participation in the process helps them to leave narrow, more self-centred considerations and moods behind. On other occasions, dislike, hostility or even hatred towards another person in the group may diminish and even disappear, as members of the group grow to understand each other more fully and unite in the task of discernment. Changes like these take place because of the group's honest search for the leading of the one Spirit in the path of the gospel, and the resulting confidence, unity and peace, when they occur, are clear confirmation of the presence of that same Spirit.

(9) Ignatius and his companions formed a small group, few enough in numbers to meet and work comfortably together as a single unit. In other circumstances, however, such as a General Chapter of a religious congregation, the number of people taking part is too great for the group to be able to work easily together as a single group all the time. At least two variations in the process have been tried with some success. (a) The large group is divided into smaller groups, each of which follows the method set out here. The results of the

smaller groups' deliberations are then brought to the larger group in plenary sessions for further consideration. (b) The members of the large group elect a smaller 'core' group to represent them. A process is set up by which the members of the core group consult the members of the large group and take note of their views and feelings. This can in fact be done by setting up small groups, with one member of the core group in each, as described in (a). The final decision-making, in this case, is the responsibility of the core group as representatives of the larger group. In this form of the process, clarification of the responsibility of the core group members *vis-à-vis* the larger group is often necessary; to determine exactly, for example, in what sense they are the representatives of the members of the larger group.

GROUP CONSOLATION AND DESOLATION

So far in this book we have discussed experiences of consolation and desolation largely in the setting of an individual's life. At this point, however, it might be appropriate to say something about these movements of feeling and their effects in the context of a group.

Spiritual moods, like other kinds of moods, are contagious. One person's joy, peace or hope, anxiety, turmoil or despair can be caught by others, as easily as catching a cold. When consolation spreads through a group, the effect is good: it brings unity, confidence, peace, energy, and so on. But when one person's desolation is caught by others, the whole group can be very easily plunged into a downward, destructive spiral, from which it is not easy to escape, because each person's desolation reinforces and confirms that of the others. This is especially true when desolation goes unrecognized and first one person then another speaks and acts under the influence of an inner mood of desolation. Each word and action of this kind encourages and reinforces the next, so that the whole group seems to be living and moving in an atmosphere of turmoil, darkness, tension and bitterness. Outside families, religious communities or other communities of

108

people living in close proximity to each other are very vulnerable to this effect of group desolation. Outsiders who come into the house can perceive the signs (though these vary, of course, in proportion to the seriousness and destructive power of the desolation and the extent to which it has taken hold of the group). There is perhaps a feeling of world-weariness, even hopelessness, about the place – a sense that nothing is really worth taking trouble over; the conversation has a current of bitterness or cynicism; there is tension in the atmosphere and each member of the community seems to live closed off from the others, defensive, critical and self-justifying; in the interaction between the members of the group or community, there is perhaps guarded politeness, but little openness or warmth; much time is given to fruitless, trivial activity. Desolation is often transmitted subliminally. It may be that no one in the group or community is aware that spiritual desolation is the cause of a particular atmosphere or ethos and is affecting each person's mood and behaviour; none the less its influence is powerful and harmful to the group as a whole and to each member.

In a group that is engaged in discernment, one person's experiences of consolation and desolation can likewise have a considerable influence for good or ill throughout the group. It is therefore important that the members of the group are free to articulate their feelings openly. Once experiences of consolation and desolation are expressed, the group, under the guidance of the facilitator, can understand and reflect on the nature of what is being expressed and the direction in which the group is being moved, and can take appropriate action, so as to move with the consolation and avoid being dragged downwards by desolation. The facilitator, therefore, has a key role: to notice, by the words, images and body-language people use, the presence of consolation or desolation; and to help the group to act appropriately on the basis of this understanding. The facilitator's role is especially important in a mood of false consolation or of desolation, simply because these are potentially so misleading and damaging for the group. As in the case of an individual afflicted by these experiences, so also in a group they call for support and encouragement, as well as wise vigilance, in a facilitator. At the same time, once the members of a group are aware of the presence of false consolation or desolation, they can support and strengthen each other.

The example that we have taken in this chapter as a paradigm for communal discernment arose, in its own historical setting, in connection with a very particular, important decision with which a small group of people found themselves confronted at a critical moment of their life as a group. There is no evidence that Ignatius and his companions as a group used this method of communal discernment in other, less critical circumstances. Our reflections on that example have so far moved in the direction of using and adapting it as a framework for communal decision-making in a similar kind of setting in our own lives. That is to say, we have been reflecting on how it might be used today from time to time, when members of a group or community find themselves faced with an important decision which affects the life of the group at a critical time.

We have seen earlier in this book, however, that discernment in the life of an individual has to do, not only with those critical moments when important choices have to be made, but also with everyday matters. In this sense discernment is seen as a way of daily living rather than an extraordinary process which, like the best china, we only bring out on special occasions. It is a feature of Christian living today, however, to ask whether what is true here for an individual is also true for a group, and to search for effective ways of practising communal as well as individual discernment in everyday life.

Let us suppose, for example, that a parish Social Action group has a core team of eight members who meet once a fortnight to review and plan the various projects which the Social Action group undertakes. It would not be unusual for this core team to want to develop a process of attending to the leading of the Spirit in their own group, as a help towards carrying out their task of steering the larger Social Action group from week to week. Many large prayer groups, too, have a similar core team which has the responsibility of leading and guiding the group as a whole.

It seems to me that the example of communal discernment used by Ignatius and his companions, which has been described in this chapter, does in fact offer a process that, with adaptation, can be used for discernment of the action and leading of the Spirit in a group in the course of everyday life. All I shall do here is highlight certain features of the process that seem to be of particular importance in such week-by-week, month-by-month discernment.

(1) It is important that each member of the group that is engaged in continuing communal discernment is committed to the process and both knows and accepts the ground rules in advance. This helps to ensure a degree of openness and trust between those taking part, which, as we have seen, greatly facilitates the process. If one or more members of the group are not committed in this way, barriers and blocks can easily be created. This need for commitment and agreement to the ground rules in advance suggests that the group may need to do some preparatory work before engaging in the discernment process.

(2) If the discernment group is part of a larger group or community (as for instance a core team or a representative council or committee would be), it is also important that the larger group, which is in some sense led or represented by the smaller group, also gives its consent to the process.

(3) Agreement about the meaning and limits of confidentiality is also an important consideration. This aspect of the ground rules enhances the freedom of the members of the group to speak openly.

(4) It is often helpful in communal discernment in daily life if the group agrees upon a future date at which the process will be evaluated and possibly modified or even discontinued. This enables members of the group to commit themselves to it

111

for a limited period of time, and then to continue or withdraw, according to what seems best.

(5) All the basic elements of communal discernment have a place here: the fundamental aim of attending to the presence and action of the Spirit; regular prayer throughout the process, nourished directly or indirectly by biblical texts; communication with a wider group of people, either because they have a particular expertise or because their lives are likely to be affected by the outcome of the discernment process; acquiring and pooling information with regard to the circumstances about which choices have to be made; willingly sharing with each other experiences of consolation and desolation and other considerations that are relevant to the discernment process; sensitivity to the movements of consolation and desolation of the group as a whole; and when a decision is being or has been made, noticing and appreciating signs of confirmation or its opposite.

CONCLUSION

In this chapter we have examined the form of group discernment used by Ignatius Loyola and his companions in 1538/9 to make a decision about their future as a group. We have seen that the process they used transfers to a group setting the essential features of a form of individual discernment developed by Ignatius in previous years and set out in *The Spiritual Exercises*. I have suggested that this form of discernment, with appropriate adaptations, offers for us today a process of group discernment in which all the members of a group have a part to play. It is a form of communal decision-making which can be used both to give shape and direction to the ongoing life of a group and on those less frequent occasions when especially important choices have to be made. In the course of the chapter I have indicated some ways in which the process is being adapted to changing circumstances. Further adaptations are also clearly possible, while at the same time we preserve the essential features of Christian discernment and ensure that each member of a group or community plays an appropriate part in the process.

1   For a fuller discussion of this see chapter 9.
2   Cf. Jules Toner's study of the 'Deliberations of the First Fathers' in 'A Method for Communal Discernment of God's Will', *Studies in the Spirituality of Jesuits*, vol. 3, no. 4 (September 1971).
3   Besides Toner's essay (note 2) see also John C. Futrell, *Making an Apostolic Community of Love* (Institute of Jesuit Sources, St Louis 1970), especially pp. 122–123.

8

Obstacles in discernment

Although discernment is concerned with choices, it reaches beyond the level of action. As we have seen, it allows the Spirit of God to shape not only our actions but also our 'hearts', the centre from which those actions flow. By responding in daily life to the call of the Spirit, we are allowing God's will to be done in us, and thus allowing the Spirit to transform us and recreate us in the image and likeness of God. We are on a journey towards being what God would have us be, towards the 'fullness of life'.

It does not come as any surprise that in joining in the dance to the music of the Spirit we meet hindrances in ourselves and in relation to the world around us. All our noblest aspirations and best activities are limited, often severely so, by factors in our make-up, our circumstances and our culture that tend to hinder the transforming work of grace. This chapter will describe some of the more serious obstacles that may impair our practice of discernment and the growth that it fosters.[1]

PHYSICAL FACTORS

The human person is fundamentally a unity. Health or disorder in one area of human life is likely to affect many other areas. When we are looking at the factors which are likely to impair discernment, it would be a mistake to confine our attention to so-called 'spiritual' obstacles, because the realm of the spirit is not a separate area cut off from other dimensions of life. All the different dimensions of human existence

114

are interconnected and interact, so that physical or psychological factors are as likely to cause obstacles in discernment as theological or spiritual factors.

Chronic states of tiredness or ill-health are likely to hinder that openness to the Spirit of God and to others which seems necessary for good discernment. Let us take an example. Moira is a wife and mother and a committed churchgoer. She gives much time and energy to her home, her three children, her husband and the different parish groups of which she is a member. She finds it increasingly difficult to cope with all the demands on her time and energy; she regularly feels tired and the energy she gains from the spells of rest that she takes – a few days here and there – does not last for very long. In the last year she has been ill with colds and influenza more often than ever before in her life. At the moment Moira and her husband Tony are faced with an important choice, a turning-point in their lives in fact, and are trying to make as good a choice as possible.

In these circumstances Moira's constant tiredness and propensity to illness, which appear to be the results of over-extending herself, would obviously be a hindrance to good discernment. She is likely, for example, to be too exhausted to give to the decision the careful attention that it really needs. She may be too tired and preoccupied to give time and energy to prayer. Moreover, her chronic fatigue would tend to distort her perceptions and judgement, confine her to living on the surface of life and prevent her from acting with freedom, openness and generosity of spirit towards other people whose lives are affected by the decision she and Tony have to make.

This example serves to illustrate the harmful effects in discernment of chronic tiredness or ill-health. Whether deliberately or not, Moira's unhappy condition is self-induced, though there are obviously millions of others who are forced into exhaustion or illness by circumstances which they cannot control. In all these cases, if one is looking for a way of overcoming or lessening the harmful effects of the chronic condition, the steps of acknowledging one's state of exhaustion or illness and of understanding both its causes and its likely negative effects in discernment are crucial and help to lessen its power to do harm. Refusing to recognize that one is exhausted or ill, which is not uncommon among religious people today, can be as harmful to good discernment as the burn-out or illness itself.

Time can also present an obstacle in discernment. There are obviously some occasions, particularly in a crisis, when decisions have to be made quickly, and there is no opportunity for lengthy deliberations. Not infrequently, postponing a decision in order to have more time for a lengthy deliberation would have worse consequences than deciding quickly. In these circumstances, when events force a quick decision, we have to trust that, if we use all the available means to choose well, the Holy Spirit also accepts the limitations of the situation and works within them. In another sense, time can also be an obstacle in discernment for people who find it very difficult to make decisions at all and tend to dither. In this case, having a long or open-ended period of time for discernment may produce endless and wearisome vacillations. It is often helpful, therefore, when there is the opportunity to practise careful discernment, to set a realistic time limit to the process, and to trust that the Holy Spirit will also work within that limit.

EMOTIONAL AND PSYCHOLOGICAL FACTORS

It is worth noting at the beginning of this section that in discussing the effects of different psychological states in discernment I am not including those conditions which are pathological in a strictly clinical sense. Mental illnesses and serious personality disorders obviously distort the perceptions and judgement of those who suffer from them, but they require skilled professional treatment and it is not within either my competence or the scope of this book to discuss them.

In this context, however, the question of depression, which is a common feature of modern life, is a difficult one. Psychologists differ as to what exactly depression is, its causes and where to draw the line between more or less acute anxiety and what is clinically identifiable as depression. What is important to recognize is the fact that both anxiety and depression are liable to have harmful results in a process of discernment and that the amount of harm they do varies according to how acute they are. If people suffering from acute anxiety or depression are involved in spiritual discernment, it is helpful and even necessary for them to have appropriate professional treatment for their psychological condition, in order to counteract its harmful consequences.

ATTACHMENTS AND ADDICTIONS

Though the terminology of 'disordered attachments', commonly met in the spiritual classics, seems quaint today, the reality that it refers to remains. Emotional and psychological 'attachments' to persons, places, objects or experiences cover a broad spectrum. They range from sentimental attachments to an old armchair, through a wide variety of emotional ties, to serious addictions without which life seems to be and sometimes really is impossible for those who suffer from them. It goes almost without saying that real addictions impair decision-making to the extent that they control behaviour and deprive a person of effective freedom. Like depression, they require professional diagnosis and treatment. There is also, however, a range of emotional and psychological attachments which, while they do not strike at the very roots of personal freedom, none the less influence our perceptions and our behaviour and are likely to have a harmful effect on our attempts to make choices by way of spiritual discernment. A person, for example, might be so given to fantasy, daydreaming, popular entertainment or work that important decisions are indefinitely postponed.

These attachments are likely to affect a process of discernment in another way. Suppose, for example, that a group of 'apostolic' religious sisters, faced with falling numbers, hold a chapter to determine their priorities in ministry for the next five years. This involves the question of what to do with the 'mother house': a large building in which they all made their novitiate and which they have collectively owned, lived in and extended for more than a hundred years. They try to approach this decision in a context of assiduous prayer with minds as open as possible as to the outcome. All I want to do here is to point out that one of the important factors in that decision is the strength of the emotional attachment (or, it may be, bitterness) of the individuals in the group towards that house. Some of them may not initially be aware that they have any strong feelings in the matter, until they surface in discussion. More important, however, is the recognition that their feelings, whether of love or hatred towards the house, can impair their freedom to follow the leading of the Spirit.

RIGIDITY IN ATTITUDES

Let us take now an illustration of a different and fairly prevalent psychological factor which is likely to impair good discernment. Jack is a middle-aged man who thinks proudly of himself as a true patriot and a staunch Roman Catholic. He thinks the country began to go to the dogs when immigrants were allowed to come in and 'take our jobs'. On Sundays he attends a Latin Mass where possible; when that is not possible, he stays at the back of the church and does not take any active part in the liturgy. A former seminarian, he read a lot of theology in the early 'sixties and believes that Vatican II has largely had a baleful influence on the church and on society generally. Before then, what it meant to be a Catholic was clear, and Jack likes clarity and good order. In discussions with his family and friends about politics or religion he tends to be defensive, immovable and self-opinionated.

As I have described him, Jack belongs to the right in politics and religion. But the left also has its devotees who are equally dogmatic and unpersuadable. And though Jack is a layman, he also has his counterparts among the clergy, and among the young clergy as well as those of his own generation.

118

Discernment, as we have seen, requires a degree of freedom, an ability to arrive at the truth by listening to others in genuine dialogue, and a good measure of openness to real change. What impedes discernment in people such as Jack, therefore, is the fact that, whatever their opinions, they hold on to them rigidly and immovably and are deaf to whoever opposes them. Whatever the psychological origin of their state, they appear to be trapped in attitudes and a view of the world and the church that are very limited and do not admit of change. It can therefore be difficult for them to give careful consideration to the views or options which are markedly different from their own. Experience of spiritual direction suggests that talking honestly to a trusted friend about their views, their anxieties and their fears can be helpful to people like Jack. It can serve to lighten the burden which they carry, and when trust has been established, those who suffer from this kind of rigidity become more easily able to see the value in attitudes and convictions which differ from their own.

LACK OF IMAGINATION

Imagination has many facets. It is often thought to belong uniquely to artists, poets, novelists, prophets and suchlike, but it is in fact a creative quality of mind and heart that is essential to every field of human activity and endeavour. Imagination is particularly important in discernment, because to take part in discernment, as we have seen, demands an ability to enter with sympathy and understanding into the minds and circumstances of other people, and the capacity both to envisage and to help to create alternatives to the present or the past. God is endlessly imaginative, and the function of discernment is to enter creatively into God's vision for the world and to collaborate with the Spirit in making that vision a reality. One of Jesus' favourite modes of teaching was by means of parables and other stories, which appeal to the imagination and give it the freedom to work and to range widely on behalf of the reign of God. Prophets are people of imagination, because they see how things could be other and better than they are and devote themselves heart and soul to the task of bringing those alternatives into existence.

Failure or inability to make use of our imagination impedes discernment. Imagination is a capacity for arriving at the truth. When there is no appeal to the imagination, or the imagination is not able to work freely and to range widely, then we are likely to be trapped within the limits of one way of looking at things, and unable to tune in when the Spirit calls for a vision of how things can be different and for change. If our imagination is stifled, then in working with other people, we tend to be unable or unwilling to listen to their viewpoints and to enter sympathetically and sensitively into their thoughts and feelings. All of this limits our capacity for good discernment, because it hinders us from recognizing the value of options and possibilities which offer us alternative ways of acting, alternative but none the less valid ways being disciples of Jesus and of struggling to make the reign of God a living reality.

FRAGMENTATION

The Western religious culture by which many of us have been formed has adopted a very negative attitude towards certain kinds of feeling, and the consequences of this attitude can be a hindrance in discernment. We can identify two strands in our religious culture which have contributed to this attitude. In the first place, we have been influenced by a tendency to condemn unbridled – or even semi-bridled – expressions of feeling. The British tradition of the 'stiff upper lip' and the code of behaviour which forbade even lovers to let each other know what they were really feeling epitomize this tendency, though in an extreme form which easily lends itself to caricature. The sight on television of Arab women wailing loudly and tearing at their hair and faces in grief still seems strange to a culture that has set such value on control of one's emotions. Obviously control of feelings is necessary for civilized life, but our culture, as Freud recognized, has tended to go beyond control to repression. The second influence which has formed us is the labelling of certain feelings as negative and the ban on expressions of them: anger, aggression, resentment, jealousy, envy, greed, and so on.

In certain Christian contexts this has led to unforeseen consequences, one of which is a conviction that not only are certain types of feeling not to be expressed, but also that having the feelings themselves is morally wrong and inadmissible. Many religious people, therefore, with the best of intentions, squashed their 'forbidden' feelings so successfully that after a time they no longer experienced them consciously. The feelings went underground, and though they covertly continued to influence people's behaviour, it was an unconscious influence. Many religious people, therefore, lost touch with their true feelings. They had repressed them to such an extent that they were no longer aware of what feelings they had.

Once again, an example will illustrate this. Father Frank is a Roman Catholic priest in his early thirties. As a young seminarian with little experience in the ways of the Spirit, it was impressed upon him that in the life of the spirit feelings were unimportant and not to be trusted. Their voice, he was told, was the voice of selfish desire and egoism, which had to be conquered. As a young man he was hot-tempered, and was constantly criticized for outbursts of anger, which he eventually learned to stifle. Those who were responsible for his formation in the seminary discouraged discussion of celibacy, relationships and sexuality, and though Frank learned to control his sexual feelings, their presence and their latent power often made him feel uneasy. He is a devoted and conscientious priest. In his pastoral ministry, however, people find it difficult to relate to him in a warm and relaxed way. While recognizing his devotedness, they find him 'living too much in his head', and unable to enter sympathetically into their concerns and their lives. They also find him rather unpredictable in his responses to them: they never know whether he is going to be sympathetic and willing to give them time, or on the other hand sharp and irritable in his reactions.

It is apparent how Frank's condition, and that of others like him, both men and women, would be likely to block good discernment. As we have described it in this book, good discernment involves allowing the whole of oneself to enter into a process of decision-making. Unfortunately, because he has been taught, for one reason or another, to hide and even repress certain 'unacceptable' feelings, Frank is not fully present either to himself or to others. There are areas of his own affective life of which he is unaware or even afraid, though in fact they influence his conduct without him being conscious of it. If he mistrusts or discounts his feelings, or if he is unaware of what he feels, he will not be able to recognize and sift the affective experiences of what we have been calling consolation and desolation. His choices, at a conscious level, are likely to be based entirely on what he finds in his head, and his discernment will tend to be distorted by needs and feelings which, though he is unaware of them, have a powerful influence on his conduct.

That is not to say, of course, that only completely integrated people, who have reached a state of fully rounded wholeness, are capable of good discernment. None the less, a lack of a certain degree of presence to oneself, a lack of awareness of the full range of one's desires and feelings and of acceptance of one's whole self, are considerable impediments to discernment. They also clearly diminish God's handiwork, because they fragment us and impede the Spirit's work of drawing us to wholeness.

In fact, of course, no one is wholly integrated. The journey towards wholeness is a long one, and the Holy Spirit works with us at whatever stage on it we happen to be. None the less, one of the ways in which the Spirit draws us towards wholeness is by challenging us to face the dark and broken side of ourselves. That step in itself, the willingness to recognize that in some sense we are fragmented, is a movement towards healing and wholeness. Once that step is made, the Spirit can work more easily in us.

IMAGES OF SELF

The images we have of ourselves can also be powerful psychological hindrances to openness and sensitivity to the Spirit of God. Whatever the situation in the past, a negative image of oneself is more likely today among Christians than one which is overblown or conceited. A 'negative self-image' means that we are habitually, though often unconsciously, unable to accept ourselves as we really are. Rather than seeing ourselves with a steady, realistic gaze and accepting ourselves as created by God with a purpose and loved by God unconditionally, one of two things happens. On the one hand we may constantly see ourselves as if in distorting mirrors which reflect back to us an image of ourselves as ugly, inept, a failure or in so many ways inferior to others. As a result, we habitually undervalue ourselves and see ourselves as being of little intrinsic worth, while we imagine that almost everyone else is more beautiful, more valuable, more capable or better endowed with all the qualities which we value so much and find wanting in our poor selves. On the other hand, even when we do know ourselves more realistically, a lack of self-acceptance may still incline us to undervalue ourselves and to have little confidence in our own gifts and capabilities, especially in comparison with what we see in others.

This lack of self-acceptance may include oneself as a whole, or it may direct attention at different times on various parts of oneself. We may focus our rejection on, for example, the body and its appearance, our gifts of mind and heart (or supposed lack of them), certain ways of behaving, particular tendencies and inclinations in ourselves that we dislike, or situations in which we feel we failed miserably. Each of these may be rejected as unacceptable.

In the context of discernment, distorted self-perception or a lack of ability to accept one's real self work destructively in different ways. They give rise, for instance, to a habitual feeling of discontent with oneself (and with the world at large), because nothing is ever quite right, nothing is ever quite good enough. They also lead to a sense of failure or to feelings of envy and jealousy, because other people always seem to have a better deal, to be more gifted, more healthy, more beautiful, more wealthy and so on. All of this means that perceptions and judgements about oneself, about other people and about situations are distorted and unreliable, because they are coloured by an ever-present, albeit unconscious, rejection.

Laura is a religious sister. She was the fourth child in a family of seven. Her father died when she was thirteen and for the next six years she helped her mother to bring up the younger children in the family. After joining her religious congregation at the age of nineteen, she spent most of her life working as a primary school teacher, moving every few years from school to school when the Provincial asked her to do so. All her other novitiate companions were trained as secondary school teachers; several of them have become head teachers and one of them is currently Provincial Superior. Though she is now slightly overweight and dresses rather dowdily, as a novice she was very slim and good-looking and took more care over her appearance until one day the director of novices reprimanded her for her 'vanity'. This year she has been elected for the first time to the Provincial Chapter of her congregation, and on the agenda are several decisions which have important consequences for the future of the congregation. The chapter turns out to be an unhappy experience for Laura. During it, to her surprise, she finds herself filled with almost uncontrollable feelings of anger, resentment and jealousy towards certain other members of the group, especially her contemporaries and some younger sisters. Her behaviour in the chapter is defensive and aggressive by turns. She also finds it difficult to pray, because she is angry with God, and throughout the chapter a cloud of pessimism and even despair about the future of the congregation seems to envelop her.

Though Laura is a religious sister, she has parallels among both men and women in every walk of life. In her present state, her capacity for good discernment is greatly impeded. Her perceptions of herself, of her own worth and of other people close to her, are distorted, and for her to act out of her present feelings would be destructive. Her ability to respond to God and to others in trust and freedom is severely impaired. If she had a friend or guide who could help her to reflect gently on her images of God and of herself in relation to God, Laura might then be able to recognize the distortions in her perceptions and come to know the God of unfailing love more fully.

FEAR

Perhaps the most powerful psychological obstacle in discernment is fear. We are not here concerned with the psychological roots of fear, which may be many and varied, but rather with its consequences. Almost anything can be for someone at some time an object of fear. There is fear of the past and of the future; fear of God and of other people; fear of stability and of change; fear of one's inner feelings and of the external world; fear of the new and of the old; fear of moving and fear of standing still; fear of speaking and fear of being silent; fear of failure and fear of success; fear of authority and fear of anarchy. Fear makes us rigid in our opinions and attitudes; fear of other people distorts our behaviour; fear of ourselves leads us to hide from ourselves and from God; fear of risk leads to procrastination and indecisiveness; fear of change or variety paralyses imagination and creativity.

Fear hinders discernment in a variety of ways. Discernment, as we have seen, demands a fair measure of peaceful openness towards the outcome of a process of decision-making, whatever that outcome may be. Those taking part in it are encouraged to approach God with an attitude of 'Thy will be done.' Fear, on the other hand, can lead us to want to control and manipulate a process in order to ensure an acceptable result. The process of discernment also demands a sifting of one's feelings towards God and in relation to certain options under consideration. Some individuals, however, might be very fearful of certain kinds of feeling such as anger which they find in themselves, and thus be hindered from acknowledging and expressing what they truly feel. Discernment, moreover, especially in the context of a group, asks those taking part to express their thoughts and feelings openly and honestly. But if I am very fearful of other people and need to maintain their high opinion of me, I am likely to be tempted to mask my true thoughts and feelings. This may be especially so if I imagine, rightly or wrongly, that what I say or do will be unacceptable to those whose approval is important to me. Furthermore, the ability to listen with openness to other people's views and feelings in the context of genuine dialogue is also essential to good discernment. An individual might be so fearful of the opinions of others, however, that his or her ability to listen to them and accept what they say is severely blocked. Discernment, finally, is also a process of making choices. Some people, however, are so fearful of choices or of taking initiatives that their discernment is seriously impeded. Either they feel an insurmountable pressure to maintain the status quo, or they find themselves simply incapable of making and carrying through a decision. They look, perhaps, for a level of assurance and certainty that can never be attained and are in danger of being paralysed by fear of taking risks.

Fear, especially fear of God or of doing wrong, also generates guilt. There is a world of difference between acknowledging due responsibility for sin and being tormented by irrational and unhealthy feelings of guilt, generated by fear and anxiety. If our dealings with God are dominated by fear rather than by love, irrational or disproportionate feelings of guilt appear in various forms. We may imagine, for instance, that we have 'offended' God by some perfectly innocent or innocuous action or omission. On the other hand, if we are aware of having done wrong, fear is likely to exaggerate the wrong so that disproportionate feelings of guilt arise to torment us. Some people, also, are driven by guilt because they are mistakenly convinced that they must strive harder and harder to do good, in order to 'make up' (to God and to others) for all the supposed wrong that they have done.

Guilt feelings of this kind hinder good discernment on several counts. True discernment is a response of love to God's love, a response made in freedom, not forced by fear or guilt. Irrational and objectively groundless guilt feelings

126

tend to distort our perceptions and our judgements of our-selves, of others and of the circumstances in which we are placed. Feelings of guilt, whether overt or hidden, can drive us into making choices, adopting or abandoning courses of action, under the mistaken impression that we are doing God's will in love and freedom. The effect of these guilt feelings is particularly harmful when they are unconscious: when they are affecting our thoughts, feelings and actions, though we are unaware of them and of their influence. Let us suppose, for example, that Peter is a young man who experiences a conversion. In a period of grace and self-discovery, he sees that so much of his past life has been irresponsible, wasteful, manipulative, unjust and so on. He believes that God is rightly angry with him. He is convinced that God is calling him to become a priest; in that way he will make amends for his past. Though he finds the road long and hard, he struggles and perseveres to ordination. In this case it is quite possible that Peter's life after his conversion is dominated by imper-fectly understood feelings of guilt. This dominance is likely to continue until he learns more about a God who forgives without conditions and calls us to be God's children in love and freedom, not slaves living in fear.

SOCIAL AND CULTURAL FACTORS

Another area in which factors appear whose influence is detrimental to good discernment is that of our individual or collective attitudes towards the society and culture which has formed us and in which we live. We are capable, for example, of certain kinds of cultural, political and ideological blindness. Political and social systems and ideologies, whether of the left, the centre or the right, tend to seduce and enslave those who benefit materially from them and those who hope to do so. Strange as it may seem, wealthy, middle-class people, who live in the more affluent areas of Latin American, African or Asian cities, can spend a whole lifetime denying or ignoring the fact that millions of others live in the same city in shanty towns in subhuman conditions of abject poverty, eking out their survival by stealing or rummaging on the city's rubbish dumps. Either they organize their lives in such a way that they never actually see the poor and the places where they live; or they are so entrapped by the dominant political and social ideology which creates these conditions that they are incapable of challenging it. They therefore either deny the existence of the poor, or justify the status quo both to themselves and to others and thus never address issues of injustice, inequality and oppression. Nor is this kind of blindness confined to the so-called Third World. A similar kind of blindness is one of the legacies of the Thatcher years in Britain. Even in the midst of increasing inner-city decadence and neglect, right-wing politicians and commentators took pains to tell the public over and over again, on the one hand that poverty and the poor do not exist in Britain, or on the other hand that if people are poor, it is through their own fault. Thus they absolve themselves and their kind from any responsibility.

The same thing also happens on a world-wide scale. The world contains both the wealth and the technology to provide adequate food and shelter for all the earth's poor. The powerful nations, however, have such a vested interest in maintaining the present economic system and its underlying ideology that they do not address the practical questions of how to provide food and shelter for those who have too little or none at all.

Obviously such attitudes as these, whether on a large or a small scale, are a block to good discernment. When we are trapped within our own political and social ideologies and systems and make them absolute instead of relative, we tend to be unable to question or challenge them and to admit the possibility or the value of alternatives. When this happens, our ideologies and systems control us, rather than the other way round, and thus deprive us of our freedom. One of the beauties of the Christian gospel, however, is its ability to question every ideology and every political system. And discernment, in the sense in which we have been using the term in this book, means precisely allowing the word of God to challenge our ideologies and our systems, and in this way to free us from their control.

THEOLOGICAL FACTORS

We saw in añ earlier chapter of this book that good discernment presupposes a God who loves us without conditions and wants us to enjoy our freedom. Such an image of God gives us a context of trust and security in God's unfailing and respectful love in which to exercise our freedom in the choices that we make. When God is imagined predominantly in other terms, however, as an inflexible lawmaker and judge, for example, as a harsh taskmaster, as a moody tyrant arbitrary in his exercise of power, as an over-indulgent parent whose love and care are unreliable, and so on, these images evoke a different kind of resonance in us: instead of love, hope, trust and confidence, they inspire fear, guilt, anxiety, isolation, despondency and discouragement. These images impede discernment by taking from us the confidence in God's love on which we depend, with the result that striving anxiously to please and win the love of a fearsome or careless God dominates any choices we make.

A view of the church which gives undue weight to authority can likewise paralyse any process of discernment. Authority obviously has a rightful place in the church; it also has limits. If my theological outlook is such that I have a slavish or infantile attitude to church authority, or if in effect I hand over to those who exercise authority, whether locally or universally, the responsibility for choices which I myself ought to make by the exercise of my own freedom, then my capacity to respond effectively to the Spirit of God is severely impaired. When 'decision-making' means no more than finding an authoritative statement which seems to meet the case and applying it to the letter, irrespective of other considerations, then each 'decision' taken in this way is a denial of the rights and the power of my own conscience and an evasion of personal responsibility. If from its consequences the decision turns out well, it reinforces my uncritical devotion to authority; if on the other hand it turns out badly, I have the satisfaction of knowing that I did exactly as I was told to do, however painful the ensuing 'cross'. In either case, this way of making decisions does not help my growth in responsible discipleship, for the reason that it impairs the use of God's gift of personal freedom.

A lack of a truly catholic theological outlook also tends to impair both our capacity for good discernment and, as a consequence, our ability to become the people God created us to be. By 'catholic' here, of course, I do not mean 'Roman Catholic'. A catholic outlook in theology is one which allows us to treat with due seriousness the whole of the Christian tradition in its many varied aspects, and the traditions of non-Christian religions also. Secondly, it is an outlook in which particular importance is given to those beliefs and practices in the Christian tradition which have been more universally accepted by the members of the church, by the *sensus fidelium*. And a truly catholic outlook also recognizes the fact that traditions both of belief and practice develop and change through time and place, since the living Spirit of God is at work in the whole church. The opposite of a genuinely catholic theological outlook, therefore, is one that is static, rigid and effectively sectarian; ready to recognize as valid only selected parts of the whole tradition or rejecting the possibility of development and change in belief and practice.

The main reason why a lack of a genuinely catholic theological outlook impairs discernment is that, explicitly or by implication, it imposes restrictions on the presence and activity of the Spirit of God. To be truly catholic means to accept that the Spirit is present and active in all times and in all places. The absence of a catholic outlook implies a conviction that certain times or places, in the past, present or future, lack the presence of the Spirit. A person with an exclusivist attitude to non-Christian religions, for example, might put forward the view that explicit recognition of Jesus as saviour is the only way to salvation; or reject the idea that the sacred texts of the great world religions apart from Christianity embody the work of the Spirit. Similarly those with a sectarian Christian outlook will admit that the Spirit is at work only in his or her own church or community, and will reject any suggestion that outsiders, 'the other side', might possess and live by the Spirit of God. Today, moreover, biblical fundamentalism, which rejects modern critical approaches to biblical interpretation and accepts as valid only a narrowly literal interpretation of the biblical texts, is a powerful opponent of a truly catholic theological outlook. These may seem to be extreme examples, but they serve to illustrate the fact that the lack of a truly catholic outlook in theology prevents us from acknowledging that the Spirit is free to roam and to work beyond the limits which we would like to impose. In this way we run the risk of resisting the call of the Spirit.

SPIRITUAL FACTORS

Another obstacle to good discernment may lie in the area of prayer. We have seen earlier in the book that discernment requires forms of prayer that allow space for listening, for being receptive as well as active. The form of prayer that is most helpful in discernment is one which allows us to be touched by God's revelation, by God's Spirit, whether through biblical texts or through other symbols which mediate God to us. Prayer in discernment, therefore, means 'time to stand and stare'.

In the ministry of retreats and spiritual direction I often meet people who find it very difficult to allow this receptive space into their prayer. They have been taught that praying means reciting prayers or talking to God; it is for them a very busy activity. Sometimes one meets individuals who set themselves a very full schedule of prayers that they feel they must 'get through' each day, and they feel very guilty if they do not complete the task. Others keep themselves very busy in prayer because at some stage in the past they have been warned against drifting into idleness and daydreaming. And some cling rigidly to one way of praying and reject suggestions that they might actually find other ways more helpful. All of these attitudes to prayer impede discernment. In each case, though the individuals concerned are trying to pray, they are unable (or at least find it very difficult) to stop being busy and to allow themselves the necessary space and silence to receive what God has to say to them.

Prayer which stays 'in the head' and never engages one's feelings also makes discernment difficult. The reasons for that are obvious. The practice of discernment, as we have discussed it in this book, involves noting and sifting the feelings that arise in response to symbols which mediate God to us. Prayer which contains space for listening, for being receptive, is a privileged setting in which these affective responses can arise. Prayer which stays in the head and never engages the heart blocks movements of consolation and desolation or alternatively hides them from view. One of the values of skilled spiritual guidance is that it helps us to move from the head to the heart, and thus towards greater wholeness.

HANDLING OBSTACLES[2]

Readers who have persevered so far with this chapter might well be feeling very pessimistic by now. Honest readers will have recognized the presence of at least one of these blocks in themselves, and many are likely at this stage to be asking: if there are so many blocks and pitfalls, how is good discernment possible for anyone? I will end this chapter by sketching a way of approaching this question.

In the face of these obstacles, the first step is an attitude of deep trust in God. God knows our limitations better than we do ourselves. If we undertake discernment with as much openness, good faith and honesty as we can muster, we can be confident that God can and will bring our efforts to a good conclusion, though it may not always be the conclusion we expect.

A second requirement is to expect blocks and obstacles to appear and therefore to be prudently on the watch for them. This is not just because everyone suffers from limitations and personal bias but because of the nature of discernment itself. It is an activity which challenges us to reach into the depths of our hearts; it uncovers our most fundamental desires and dispositions and the features of our most basic relationships: with God, the world and ourselves. In that setting one would expect resistances and blocks to show themselves.

A third requirement when blocks do appear, whether in individual discernment or in a group process, is to acknowledge and address them as well as one can. Sometimes the very fact of being able to recognize and acknowledge an obstacle in discernment takes us a long way towards overcoming it. Sometimes, if hindrances are addressed with a little well-directed effort, they can be removed or surmounted. Other blocks, however, are more or less permanent features of our personal lives and circumstances, and any attempt to be rid of them is a long-term task with no assurance of success even then. In these cases, if we acknowledge the difficulty, try to address it and take into account its influence on the discernment process, we can be confident that God can bring the process to a good conclusion.

Discernment, as we have often seen, demands a measure of effective personal freedom on the part of the individuals who have responsibility for making choices. The most precious freedom that we have is the freedom to know God and in the light of that knowledge to become the people that God created us to be. This freedom in any case is never absolute; it is always limited by factors within and external to ourselves. The most serious blocks to good discernment are those which hinder this freedom to such an extent that it is no longer effective, or which deprive us of it altogether. This occurs when our choices and our actions are in fact in the control, not of the free human spirit but of some other agency, be it physical, emotional, psychological, social, theological or spiritual. There is no block that is totally resistant to the Spirit of God. Guided and supported by grace, once the human spirit recognizes the nature of the obstacles with which it has to contend, it often finds ways of asserting its right to freedom, even in the face of the most daunting hindrances.

When we try to address the obstacles that we discover in ourselves, the presence of another person is often extremely helpful and even necessary. Sometimes the obstacles are a matter of the limitations of our knowledge or education, and can be overcome relatively easily. On the other hand, a skilled counsellor or therapist will show the way towards recognizing and dealing with the emotional and psychological blocks that we have been discussing. In all cases, however, a 'soul-friend' or spiritual guide will also be of great assistance. This person's role is precisely to help another to reflect upon his or her own life in the context of faith and in relation to God. Inevitably, sooner or later, when the time is right, this process involves recognizing those things which cause blocks in relation to God and others and impede the growth towards wholeness. When these blocks are recognized and shared, they can be addressed in a setting of faith and trust.

1   This chapter owes much to Margaret Goldsbury's article, 'Blocks to Discernment', in *The Way Supplement*, no. 64 (Spring 1989), pp. 80–87.
2   On ways of dealing with blocks and resistances in spiritual direction, see *The Practice of Spiritual Direction* by William A. Barry and William J. Connolly (Seabury Press, New York 1983), ch. 6; and *Women at the Well* by Kathleen Fischer (SPCK 1989), chs. 7–10; *Soul Friend* by Kenneth Leech (Sheldon Press, London 1977), ch. 3.

9

Dialogue with the tradition

The practice of discernment that I have described in this
book belongs to the tradition of discernment and spiritual
guidance that stems from Ignatius Loyola. It represents a
modern rediscovery, interpretation and adaptation of the
practice bequeathed to the church by Ignatius. In this connection, two facts about Ignatius are noteworthy. The first is
that he was far more interested in the practice of discernment
than in the theory. His concerns were primarily pastoral: to
develop the skills which would enable him, as he put it, 'to
help souls'. He was interested in theory, not for its own sake,
but only in so far as it grounded and supported his practice
and enabled him to be a more effective spiritual guide. Secondly, in the matter of discernment he was a summarizer
rather than an innovator or inventive genius.

Ignatius himself, therefore, did not invent this art of discernment which he left to his successors. It came to him from
two principal sources. The story of his own life which he
narrated to Luis Gonçalves da Câmara a few years before his
death tells how Ignatius learned discernment partly through
reflection on his own experience of changes and movements
of feeling in different situations. The other source from which
he learned discernment was his reading: the tradition of
Christian discernment which he inherited from the spiritual
writers who had gone before him. His originality, if so it can
be called, lay in his skill in noting and reflecting on his own
experience, his ability to absorb from his reading whatever

would help him to interpret his and others' experience, and his gift for taking from the tradition whatever was relevant to his own circumstances. These qualities enabled him to produce an ordered set of practical steps and guidelines on discernment which other people could use, both in their own lives and as the basis for helping others to grow in the life of the Spirit. Ignatius, therefore, is a pool into which, directly or indirectly, many other streams from the past flowed. The practice of discernment that we have discussed in this book is a stream that flows out of that pool.

IGNATIUS AND THE EARLIER TRADITION

In the process of developing an art of discernment and writing guidelines for others to use, Ignatius drew plentifully upon others' writings. He was selective, however, in what he used. He used the spiritual wisdom which he inherited like a prospector panning for gold. He sifted it thoroughly through his own experience and took from it only the nuggets he wanted, letting the rest go.

It was John Cassian who was largely responsible for introducing to the western world the spirituality and way of life of the men and women who created the monastic life in the deserts of the East in the third century. He visited the desert monasteries in the second half of the fourth century and set out to explain their spirituality in his writings. Most of what medieval Europe knew of the spirituality of the desert came from him; so that it has been said of John Cassian that 'all the guides to spirituality in which western Europe later abounded were his descendants'.[1] Knowledge of Cassian's desert spirituality passed into the middle ages and thence into Ignatius' age by way of both the universities and the monasteries in several forms: in Cassian's own writings, in compilations of texts from various authors put together for different occasions and in the writings of monastics and theologians who had absorbed Cassian's spirit and made it their own.

Whether or not Ignatius actually read Cassian's writings

or received his teaching indirectly through others, the spirituality of the desert seems to have had a strong appeal for him. It is as though he felt an intuitive affinity with the spirit and way of life of those early monastics, and in a sense that is not wholly surprising. Ignatius' experiences at Manresa and his pilgrim years were not unlike the formative periods of solitude in remote desert places undergone by Antony and others. Later he kept up close connections with the Carthusians and for a time considered taking up their eremitical life. Like the desert hermits, Ignatius also needed to develop a practice of personal discernment, because for some years he was a solitary pilgrim bent on discovering his own path of discipleship. Moreover, the wholehearted commitment evoked by Ignatius' Spiritual Exercises bears a close resemblance to the 'purity of heart' sought by the women and men of the desert. Both Cassian and Ignatius saw a union of will with God as the aim of the spiritual quest; and both emphasized the importance of desires in that quest. Furthermore, for both men, a continuous confrontation with evil was an inevitable part of the search for authentic discipleship (Exx 136–148), though Ignatius and his companions experienced this as taking place for them 'in the world' more than in the solitude of the desert.

To these likenesses between Ignatius' approach and that of the monastic men and women of the desert we can add the fact that the way of life that Ignatius instituted represented a break with contemporary conventional forms of Christian life, as did that of the desert monastics. The early Jesuits moved away from established patterns of 'religious life' into 'pilgrim' circumstances where, having no monastic framework of large communities, stability, a regular pattern of life, the communal Divine Office and chapter government, they had to rely heavily on their own individual inner resources in order to be faithful to their calling. And in fact many of the very early Jesuits were virtually solitaries: not hermits in the desert but travelling evangelists like Francis Xavier and Pierre Favre. Their house, according to their companion Jerome Nadal, a trusted interpreter of Ignatius, was 'the road'. Additionally, both the role of the one who gives the Spiritual Exercises and the role of the superior as outlined in the Jesuit Constitutions, especially in regard to the formative years, closely resemble that of the spiritual mother or father in the desert tradition. In fact, it could be argued that the programme of formation set out in the Jesuit Constitutions is a formation for apostolic solitaries. Its structures embody the hope that, having been through the programme, a man is so proficient in personal discernment that, in occasional consultation with his superior or spiritual director, he can make decisions about his personal life and about mission which reflect the values of 'discerning love' embodied in the Spiritual Exercises. Furthermore, outside the circle of the members of his order, many of those whom Ignatius helped with discernment were lay people and bishops in often lonely positions of responsibility and influence. His letters show him assisting them to make personal choices about the use of their wealth and power in situations where very probably, in order to be able to put into practice the values of the gospel, they often had to resist the wisdom of their peers and entourages and stand alone. Ignatius 'loved large cities' (*magnas amavit urbes*) and transposed the spirituality of the desert into the marketplace and into the palaces of the great.

THE PROTESTANT PRINCIPLE

Through his studies in Paris and his later evangelizing activities, Ignatius was in touch with the events and the controversies of the Reformation. Some of the early Jesuits were involved in the Council of Trent and in official dialogues between Catholics and Lutherans. Historically, since the Reformation, Catholics and Protestants have emphasized different elements of ecclesial life. Here, it should be noted, we are talking not about two different churches, but about two different but interrelated outlooks or traditions of thought and action. Catholics, for example, have stressed the importance of orthodoxy in doctrine, universal norms in ethics and spirituality, the necessity of regular sacramental practice, the efficacy of the sacraments as means of grace irrespective of the spiritual and moral state of those who are responsible for 'administering' them, and the presence of the Holy Spirit in the hierarchy and structures of the church. Protestants, on the other hand, have placed greater value on such matters as contact with the Bible as the word of God, personal experience, freedom and responsibility in ethics and spirituality, personal conversion and commitment to Christ, personal faith seen as total adherence in trust to God and the presence of the Spirit in the hearts and minds of individuals.

Though Ignatius adopted wholeheartedly the hierarchical and institutional view of the church current in the Catholic theology of his time, none the less there is also a 'Protestant principle' at work in Ignatian spirituality and Ignatian discernment.[2] Ignatius himself, as we have seen, drew much of his skill in discernment from reflection on his own experience. On more than one occasion he defended and stood by the value of his own experience and interpretation of that experience over against the demands of the Inquisition, who suspected his orthodoxy and the fact that at that time he had not gone through an approved course of theological study. The process of the Spiritual Exercises encourages and stimulates a personal conversion and commitment to Christ, the features of which bear some resemblance to those described and advocated by Evangelical Protestants.

Although Ignatius loved and worked hard to renew the Catholic church to which he belonged unswervingly, none the less Ignatian spirituality is attractive to those who belong to the Protestant traditions partly because of the attention he gives to personal discernment.[3] In fact, there is a sense in which Ignatian discernment is a 'Protestant' activity. That is because the Ignatian tradition recognizes the importance in the Christian life of personal searching, personal appropriation of the biblical word of God, heartfelt conversion and individual commitment to Christ as the basis of Christian discipleship. Moreover, Ignatian discernment encourages people to use the biblical word of God to reflect on their own history and experience, and it leads them to make personal judgements and choices based on that reflection, precisely because the history and experience of individuals and

139

communities within the church are very important places in which the Spirit is speaking.

Ignatian discernment, however, is not a matter of setting the individual and the church over against each other, nor of naively or aggressively supporting the individual against the institution when tensions and conflict occur. As we have seen, efficacious Ignatian discernment means recognizing that the Spirit of God uses all possible means in the church (and, for that matter, outside it) to address and guide us. It means sifting through all those different forms in which God seems to come to meet us, whether they are personal or institutional, in order to shape our lives and our world in accordance with God's desires. In that respect, therefore, Ignatian discernment seeks to unite the best of both 'Catholic' and 'Protestant' tendencies in Christianity.

There is another way, too, in which a 'Protestant' principle operates in Ignatian spirituality and discernment. We have seen that effective discernment involves giving due scope and weight to both the intellectual and the affective dimensions of our existence. Here too, since the Reformation, there have been quite marked differences of emphasis between Catholics and Protestants. The Catholic tradition has stressed the importance of the mind in the Christian life and thereby failed in some ways to give due emphasis to the affective side of human living. This tendency can be seen in several areas. Catholicism has insisted that true knowledge and the right action that flows from it are necessary for salvation. Catholics and Protestants have thus differed in their understanding of what faith is. For Catholics faith has been seen predominantly as 'the faith': a coherent system of doctrines which all who belong to the church are expected to believe and where necessary to defend. Protestants, on the other hand, have tended to view faith as personal adherence in trust to God and to Christ. And while Catholics have insisted on right knowledge, Protestants, by contrast, have tended to focus on such matters as trustful dependence upon Christ as the only saviour, the place of religious feeling in the Christian life, and affective change as a sign of the validity of personal conversion.

The Ignatian tradition of spirituality, therefore, can claim a 'Protestant' principle in the way in which it highlights the place of feeling in the Christian life. In Ignatian discernment, as we have seen, human feeling is not something to be ignored, denied or crushed in one's relationship with God, but rather an important and integral factor. Discernment in the Ignatian tradition is 'Protestant' in that certain desires and feelings are seen both as signs of a genuine conversion and commitment to Christ, and as pointers towards where the Spirit is at work. Ignatian discernment welcomes feeling and restores the partnership of mind and heart.

INFLUENCE OF THE IGNATION TRADITION OF DISCERNMENT

At the present time there is a growing interest in the practice of Ignatian discernment, largely through the practice of individually-guided retreats, particularly among Roman Catholics, Anglicans, Methodists, Quakers and members of the Reformed Churches in English-speaking countries. This is due to what almost amounts to a rediscovery of the importance of Ignatian discernment by the Jesuits and their associates in recent years. Ignatian spirituality as a whole spread widely in the Roman Catholic church from the sixteenth century onwards, because of the numbers of Jesuits, their ubiquity and their influence. For most of that time, however, it was other features of Ignatius' legacy, rather than his guidelines on discernment, which tended to be highlighted and had the strongest appeal. Soon after Ignatius' death, the Society of Jesus began to grow increasingly institutional, a tendency which persisted well into the twentieth century. Other founders of religious congregations, particularly in the nineteenth century, adopted certain elements of Ignatius' legacy, especially his missionary emphasis, the ascetical principles and methods of meditation to be found in the Exercises (which incidentally were often given an intellectual rather than an affective slant), and the structural and institutional aspects of the Jesuit Constitutions.

As for the Spiritual Exercises, although they were widely used with great effect among Roman Catholics for four hundred years, it was not primarily because of their teaching on discernment. The Exercises tended to be seen in one of two ways; either as a school of contemplative prayer or as a manual of asceticism. And although the Exercises formed the framework of countless retreats, these largely took the form of preaching to a group or a large congregation rather than individual guidance, and in these circumstances the Exercises were quarried for ideas that could be made into a sermon or a talk.

The tradition of Ignatian discernment, however, did continue in the Roman Catholic Church, albeit as a relatively minor element in Ignatian spirituality. It was passed on at a practical level by Jesuit spiritual directors, some of whom left writings, and on a theoretical level in the theology of Francisco Suarez and his followers. But from the sixteenth century until the time of Vatican II it was seen as a relatively minor element in Ignatian spirituality. It is only in the last thirty years that discernment has been widely recognized as a key aspect of the way of Christian discipleship which Ignatius bequeathed to us.

Despite the presence of what we have called a 'Protestant principle' in Ignatian discernment, on the occasions when Ignatian spirituality has found its way into other than Roman Catholic traditions, it has not been, until very recently, because of Ignatius' teaching on discernment.[4] Here too it was other elements like Ignatius' missionary commitment, his teaching on prayer and meditation or certain structural aspects of the Jesuit Constitutions that have provided inspiration. The presence of the Jesuits in England and the availability of *The Spiritual Exercises* and other Roman Catholic books which were inspired by an Ignatian approach to prayer had an influence, for example, on seventeenth-century Anglicanism and John Donne in particular. Here it was the method and structure of the meditations and contemplations in *The Spiritual Exercises* that were found helpful. Much later John Wesley read a life of Ignatius and expressed guarded admiration for him in his diary, though Ignatius is not reckoned among the more important continental Roman Catholic influences on the growth of Wesley's spirituality. In the second half of the nineteenth century, a small number of Anglican and American Episcopalian religious congregations were formed, which to some degree were influenced by Ignatian spirituality. They were inspired by Ignatius' missionary thrust and the practice of making regular retreats, including that of thirty days, though for the most part they retained monastic or conventual structures, and the retreats tended to be 'preached' rather than in the form of individual guidance. At the end of the nineteenth century, the American Baptist pastor Walter Rauschenbusch was so impressed by the zeal of Ignatius and the 'strength and cohesion of the Jesuit order' that he founded the 'Little Society of Jesus' in 1887 to work among the urban poor. More recently there are traces of Ignatian spirituality in the continental Protestant churches. Dietrich Bonhoeffer had a (partly uncut) copy of *The Spiritual Exercises* in his library. This suggests that he may have turned to it when, in his underground seminary, he started the practice of daily scripture meditation. However, despite the fact that Ignatian spirituality found its way into Anglican and Protestant traditions, the current interest in Ignatian discernment among their present members is due largely to recent direct contact with their Roman Catholic counterparts, rather than to the presence of a continuous or widespread explicit Ignatian influence in those churches.

QUAKER DECISION-MAKING

It may come as a surprise to realize that there were marked similarities in experience and outlook between Ignatius Loyola, a Basque nobleman who became a personal acquaintance of popes, cardinals and bishops, and George Fox (1624–91), an egalitarian English shoemaker and son of a weaver, who founded the Religious Society of Friends (Quakers). Both underwent dramatic conversions which radically changed the direction of their lives but in the process also brought them, each in his own way, to the slough of despond and the edge of despair. Both spent time in prison for their religious activities. Both were opposed to the worldliness and corruption of the clergy and worked for reform, although George Fox chose a path outside the mainstream church while Ignatius worked from within it. Each of them wanted to bring the whole world to Christ. And each, believing he was led by God, founded an organization which grew rapidly and handed on to a new generation the spirit and insights of the founder.

What is perhaps most significant in our present context is the fact that each of them, independently of each other of course, evolved a method of communal discernment. Both Ignatius Loyola and George Fox believed that what Fox called 'the inner light' is present in everyone and that the Spirit of God guides us in and through the events of life and the inner movements that we experience. The methods of communal discernment that they evolved reflect that conviction. While Ignatius' practice of communal discernment was little used after 1538, the Quakers have been using a method of communal discernment in their regular meetings for business for three hundred years.[5]

The distinctive style of Quaker meeting for worship is well known: the whole group sits in contemplative silence for the whole of the agreed length of time. If anyone in the meeting feels moved to speak, he or she may do so, while the rest listen in silence. If no one feels moved to speak, the whole time passes in the same prayerful silence. The meeting for business, which uses a process of communal discernment, has the same basic structure. The numbers present are usually small. The clerk has the responsibility of conducting the meeting without dominating; this includes introducing the topics on the agenda, summarizing the 'sense of the meeting' at appropriate moments and formulating decisions and proposals. Anyone who has ideas on the subject under consideration may speak, and no one outranks anyone else. There is no voting, and when agreement cannot be reached, a moratorium is declared. The meeting begins and ends in silence. The contemplative depth and influence of this silence appear to vary, depending on the seriousness of the issues to be decided and the extent of disagreement among those present. Relatively trivial matters might be decided without recourse to lengthy periods of silence. On the other hand, if there is clear disagreement, prayerful silence will often help to bring a unity among the members which might be impossible to achieve by the more usual means of debate or argument.

Quaker and Ignatian communal discernment clearly have some features in common: the search for a profound unity of minds and hearts in the one Spirit with regard to certain choices; an emphasis on the importance of prayer; a willingness to listen and have one's views changed; a setting in which those who speak may be heard with openness and respect; a process by which conflict can be expressed and given due weight; a dislike and mistrust of emotionalism; an attempt to allow the 'inner light' to shape the speech of individuals; the possibility of stating disagreement without wishing to block the decision; a preference for voteless decision-making; a tendency to postpone the decision until a sense of unity has been reached. Quakers also report that, as in Ignatian group discernment, the method adopted sometimes leads to changes in attitude and opinion among those who take part.

SIGNS AND WONDERS

The men and women of Jesus' time were challenged to decide whether the 'signs' that he performed were of God or not. In various places and at different times in Christian history (and in the history of other religious traditions) there have been surges of interest in extraordinary experiences and events: visions, locutions, unusual mystical experiences, surprising gifts of the Spirit, apparitions and miracles: signs and wonders of all kinds. The charismatic renewal of recent years has given rise to accounts of extraordinary phenomena: among them speaking in tongues, being 'slain in the Spirit', gifts of prophecy and 'miraculous' healings. People like Padre Pio and places like Medjugorje and Lourdes have been and still are focuses of intense interest. In this book we have given our attention to the 'ordinary' rather than the 'extraordinary' in the life of Christian discipleship; though in fact what we see as 'ordinary' matters – conversion, the power of grace in everyday living, growth in the life of the Spirit, learning to

tune in to the music of the Spirit – are really quite extraordinary events.

While discernment obviously has its place in the ordinary,
what is often not recognized is that it also has a crucial part
to play when we have to deal with circumstances in which
people claim to have experience of extraordinary signs and
wonders. The occurrence of these experiences and events, of
course, raises questions for psychology, physics, medicine,
biology and other sciences about whether and how they can
be explained in scientific terms. Discernment, however, as we
have seen, is not primarily concerned with precisely those
questions. It does not set out to give a scientific explanation
of the causes of certain events or experiences or to say why
or how they occur. That is not, however, to say that in this
setting discernment has nothing to offer. On the contrary,
when we are faced with unusual and mysterious signs and
wonders, discernment is essential. It asks different but equally
important questions, and scientific evidence and information
are crucial in the process of discernment as a help towards
answering those questions.

In situations in which it is claimed that religious signs and
wonders take place, our primary need, from the point of view
of discernment and growth in the life of faith, is to 'discern
the gifts': to know the direction in which these experiences
are drawing those who have them or witness them. Are they
harmful or beneficial in terms of a relationship with God?
Are they truly creative or destructive? Are they likely to help
or hinder the search to make the reign of God a living reality?
Are they likely to assist others and ourselves towards becoming what God desires us to be, or to impede us? Do they
express what God wants for the world, or are they a distrac-
tion from it?

Given that in the presence of extraordinary religious events
and experiences these questions are most important, the kind
of discernment that we have discussed in this book has a vital
part to play. It is precisely an attempt to give an answer to
those questions. It offers, as we have seen, a way of sifting
and evaluating our experiences, however ordinary or extraordinary they may be, in the context of our relationship with

God. Whatever the experiences in question may be, the same process of noting, interpreting and evaluating experience, and the same criteria, apply.

CONCLUSION

In the Roman Catholic tradition the practice of discernment that Ignatius Loyola discovered and developed has been a constant if undervalued presence for 450 years. Sharing our spiritual gifts as well as our theology is part of the ecumenical task. At the present time we are witnessing an ecumenical convergence in Ignatian spirituality. Many Christians from all traditions are recognizing that one of their needs in the marketplace, which also has features of the desert, is a way of living which will enable them to find and to follow the leading of the Spirit in the path of the gospel; a means of tuning in to the contemporary music of the Spirit. They are brought closer together in the discovery that the form of Christian discipleship which stems from Ignatius Loyola, with discernment as a key element, offers an answer to that need.

1   *John Cassian* by Owen Chadwick (Cambridge University Press, second edition 1968), p. 162.
2   I have explored the relationship between Ignatian spirituality and the church more fully in my previous book *Eyes to See, Ears to Hear: An introduction to Ignatian spirituality* (Darton, Longman and Todd, 1990) chs. 9 and 10. On the 'Protestant principle' see Thomas A. Clarke, 'The Protestant Principle', *The Way Supplement*, no. 68 (Summer 1990), pp. 52–61.
3   See 'Why Ignatian Spirituality Hooks Protestants' by Joyce Huggett, *The Way Supplement*, no. 68 (Summer 1990), pp. 22–34.
4   For a discussion of the spread of Ignatian spirituality outside Roman Catholicism see 'The Influence of the Ignatian Tradition' by Philip Sheldrake in *The Way Supplement*, no. 68 (Summer 1990) pp. 74–85.
5   For a study of Quaker decision-making by a writer whose roots are in the Ignatian tradition see: *Beyond Majority Rule: Voteless*

decisions in the Religious Society of Friends by Michael J. Sheeran SJ (Philadelphia Yearly Meeting of the Religious Society of Friends, Philadelphia 1983). See also the same author's article 'Ignatius and the Quakers' in *The Way Supplement*, no. 68 (Summer 1990), pp. 86–97.